D0680572

Mary Frances Winters (signature)

Only Wet Babies Like Change

Workplace Wisdom for Baby Boomers

Dr. Mary-Frances Winters

Renaissance Publishers, Inc.

Springfield, Virginia

January 2002

For more information contact:
Renaissance Publishers, Inc. • P.O. Box 220096 • Chantilly, Virginia 20153
or c/o The Winters Group, Inc. • 8816 Jericho Drive,
Landover, MD 20785 • Telephone 301-336-0400.

ISBN No. 0-9673993-1-9

www.wintersgroup.com
www.Laniersbookstore.com
Cover design by Debra Atkins-Manos, A-M Creative
Cover image: Digital Imagery © 2002 PhotoDisc, Inc.

Preface

When is the book going to be finished?

This question has been posed by many friends and well wishers over the last five years. You see, I declared before a group of about 500 in 1996 that I was writing a book. It was during a keynote presentation when I half jokingly said, since I have announced it, I guess I have to do it! I asked the group to hold me to it. Well, they have been true to their word. A recent phone call to my office is an example. My assistant, Debby Russo, took the call from someone we did not know. The caller asked, "Is this the number for the Mary-Frances Winters who was going to write a book? Has the book been published? I think I remember reading someplace that she was going to be writing...a newspaper clip or something." The caller had no idea that I had just that day completed the manuscript. Debby was laughing when she relayed the message and said, "What timing, huh?" Providence? Serendipity?

Since I made that declaration in 1996, my journey has been fraught with significant life-altering experiences, the most difficult being the sudden death of my husband of 24 years in 1997. He was 47 years old.

I have learned much over these following years. I have learned that what my mother used to say about faith is true: "All you need is the faith of a mustard seed." Sometimes, that is literally all I had. I also learned that for all of the bad things that happen in life that we cannot explain, love truly does conquer all.

i

I am well loved by family and friends who span the globe. I praise God every day for my multitude of blessings. I am so very grateful.

So I must acknowledge as many of those special people as I can. For without your love, the completion of this project would not have been possible. It is important to me to list by name those who have touched me, but if I have left anyone out, forgive me.

Joseph R. Winters II and Mareisha Nicolle Winters, my precious children of whom I am most proud. Not only are they smart and motivated but more importantly, they are loving and compassionate.

Leon T. Lanier, Sr., thank you for your patience and believing in me so completely.

Lawrence A. Smith, my father, and Lawrence C. Smith, my brother, for your unconditional love. The late Gladys Smith, my mother, who showed me there is always a way. Aunt Frances, cousins Terry and George in Canada, and cousins Ora and Thelma Williams in New Jersey—all who have been steadfast.

Angeletta Winters, my mother-in-law, for loving me as your own. Lawrence, Jonetta and Romande Winters for loving me like a sister. Special mention to sister-in-law Marjorie Karim and her family for showing me the real meaning of faith. To nieces Sheron and Dawn Smith for showing me the real meaning of "against all odds."

Debby Russo, who has been my faithful and caring office assistant for 17 years, and has *always* been there for whatever I need, whenever I need it, with a bright smile and cheery outlook.

My loving goddaughter, Kenya Stewart, and my talented godson, Marcus Fugate, who bring me immense joy.

Now for the list of special friends with whom I have shared the joys, the triumphs, the trials, and the tribulations of life:

Alnita and Ester Tramell, Marcia and Tom Fugate, Gail and Carl Livingston, Bessie Valle, Deborah Dixon, Sharon Foster Adams, Joanne Weaver, Mildred Campbell, Karin Shealey, Essie Calhoun, Tina Chapman, Mary Patton, Carmen Bassett, Pamela Bradley Smith and Terry Smith, Walter Fluker, Charlotte and Dover Downing, Delores and Robert Geter, James and Deborah Goins, Jackson and Carolyn Colllins, Marie and Curtis Rivers, Zell and Ernest Hicks, Bianca and Stephen Ferguson, Peggy Harvey Lee, Carol and John Adams, Gwen Martins, Sandra Nettles, Brenda and Alan Caine, Wyoma Best, Patricia and Bob Soltys, Carol and Jesse Champ, Robert and Ann Young, Kitty Sizer, Dolores Rodriques, Joseph and Billye Mayo, Eula Bing, Pamela O'Conner-Chapman, Ken Hines, The Honorable William A. Johnson, Jr., Juliette Cummings, Denise Sawyer Johnson, Clayton Osborne, John Hill, Vernita and Emerson Fullwood, William Faucette, Sr, Melva and Larry Brown, Jean Howard, Bernice and Richard Everett, Matthew Augustine and Rita Augustine (deceased), Madeline Sulaiman-Eason, Faith Adams, Sandy Davis, Gayle Harris, Mary E. Smith, Lorraine Clement, Vikki Ray, Pamela Nesbitt-Young, and Thelma Nichols.

Carole Bilson, Josephine Tolbert Bonds, Frances Bryniarski, Bridgett Burch, Ermine Byas, Jacqueline Dobson, Jean Howard, LaMarr Jackson, Marguerite Peoples Jacobs, Loretta Dunville Johnson, Jewelle Gayle Jones, Katherine Logan, Constance Mitchell, Ruby Nelson, Virdell Robbins, Coral Surgeon, Molly Thornton, Joan Ridley Willis, Barbara Williams deLeeuw, Mary Ann Wolfe, Alice Young, Francine Conwell, Giselle Washington, Cynthia McGill, Julie Lane Hailey, Sherry Gearing, Gloria Huddleston, Theresa Jackson, Victoria Kelly, Bessie Martin, Louise Peeples, Essie Potts, Gloria Rogers, Patricia Sims, Rose Stokes, Darlene White, Dr. Dwight E. Cook, Doris Ponitz, Judith Bogart, Rev. Betty Boyd Mackey, Stella and Clayton Wiley, Thomasina and Ossie Moorehead, Beverly Freeman, and Rev. Errol and Alberta Hunt.

Those individuals I have met and benefited from spiritually and professionally, as I have developed the business over the years include:

Al Martins (deceased), Walter Cooper, William Stolze, Robert Wayland Smith, Jane Plitt, Judy Columbus, Tina Smagala, Doug McLaine, Jan Austin, John Barr, Garry Britton, Patrick Coffey, Jackie Cooper, Keith Jenkins, Betty Richardson, Jose Rivera, Charles Pfeffer, Marcus Robinson, Margaret Sanchez, Julian Puretz, Nancy Volkmuth, Sandra Simon, Frank Staropoli, Willie Weaver, Sue Wajda, Dr. Price Cobbs, Barbara Dean, Skip Hansford, Joe Laymon, and Brenda Gumbs.

Steve Hanamura, Patricia Harbour, Robert Hayles, Jeff Howard, Marilyn French and Edward Hubbard, Kay Iwata, Linda Jimenez, Judith Katz, Juan Lopez, Armida Mendez-Russell,

Julie O'Mara, Alan Richter, Sondra Thiederman, R. Roosevelt Thomas, Jr., David Tulin, Michael Wheeler, Lynda White, Jennifer Leonard, Joanne Scanlan, Betty Brentley, Emmett Carson, William Crothers, Rich Rose, Al Simone, George Fisher, Kay Whitmore, Charles Barrentine, Augustin Melendez, John Martin, Bill Wallace, Kathy Hudson, Carolyn and James Blount, May Snowden, James Sutton, Gilbert and Ken McCurdy, Dennis O'Brien, John Williams, Kenneth Howard (deceased), Betty Brownell, Nora Herbert, Rebecca Olejar, Donald Monacell, Linda Strauss-Jones, Mary Burkhardt, Daniel Meek, Len Redon, Mary Catherine Bosner, Howard Berman, Cleve Killingsworth, Stephanie Street, Cathy Brill, Pamela York-Klainer, William Castle and Carole Copeland-Thomas.

Cathy Kamp, founder and president of Creative Ink, Ltd., has struggled with me for the duration. She has edited, re-edited, conceptualized and re-conceptualized with me over the years. I truly thank you for being one of my staunchest supporters. Thanks also to Joan Matochik, Linda Zuber, and Linda Interlichia for the proofreading and research.

To all of those other wonderful souls too numerous to mention who have watched from afar, I know that you are there. I can feel the love surrounding me. Thank you.

I hope you enjoy the book.

Mary-Frances Winters

January 2002

Table of Contents

In Memory of

Joseph Richard Winters, Sr.
October 13, 1950 – November 5, 1997

Introduction

The illiterate of the 21st century will not be those who cannot read or write, but those who cannot learn, unlearn and relearn.

Alvin Toffler, Contemporary American Futurist and Author

How many times over the past 20 years have you heard your employer say, "We need to change, to be more flexible, more adaptable. The competition is formidable"? How many seminars have you been required to attend that address the transformation of the workplace, the new business and personal requirements for success? How many restructurings, management changes, and downsizings have directly or indirectly impacted you? There is no denying that the workplace has been in a state of total upheaval over the past two decades.

CHANGE! CHANGE! CHANGE! Embrace it! Love it! Be energized by it! Phooey! Let's face it. No matter how much we know that it is inevitable — that change is surely going to come, we still don't like it — even those of us who think we are enlightened, who think we thrive on change. The roller-coaster ride that the business world is experiencing is a bit much, even for the most sophisticated of change masters.

After being on this roller-coaster ride as corporate America has downsized, outsourced, re-engineered, de-layered, de-selected, divested, and otherwise totally transformed itself for more than two decades now, we are more than a little frustrated and need a reprieve. As the old saying goes, "Too much of anything 'ain't' good for nobody." No one can stay on a roller coaster for too long without feeling slightly queasy.

Literally, no business from high tech to not-for-profit has been spared. It doesn't matter if you are a hospital orderly, banker, chemical engineer, sales associate, or small business owner. You have been through significant and rapid change, and guess what? There is no end in sight.

So why do I focus on baby boomers? Everybody has experienced tremendous change. First, I'm one of the almost 80 million[1] Americans who are members of that august group born between 1946 and 1964. We make up 28 percent[2] of the population and 48 percent of the workforce.[3] I think we are the most resistant to change. We may resist change in other aspects of our lives, too, but this book is about dealing with change in your work life.

There are good reasons why baby boomers are the staunchest resistors. We started our careers in the stable industrial era and now find ourselves mid- or end-career in the chaotic knowledge era. Today's work world doesn't look much like the one in which baby boomers started their careers. In the industrial era, jobs were mostly manufacturing-related, routine, predictable, and secure. The end results were tangible products; the work itself was often physical. In the knowledge era, it is not brawn but brainpower that drives the economy. Information, innovation, and creativity have replaced coal, steel, and energy as our most valuable resources. Companies that will win the competitive race today are those that will continually reinvent themselves and produce their products and services faster, better, and smarter. Therefore, companies look for people who can constantly reinvent themselves to be a part of this winning team.

Such monumental changes have been a bitter pill for the baby boom cohort, who started their careers when the promise of lifetime employment—in exchange for hard work and loyalty—was a given.

Many of us started our careers in the heyday of the industrial age. Many enjoyed (and still do) the material benefits of job security. Too many of us spent all—or more than all—of our incomes to accrue those material comforts.

We don't save our money. According to former Harvard University economist Juliet Schor, Americans save only 3.5 percent of their disposable income—one-quarter of what the French, Italians, Japanese, and Germans save.[4] When it comes to baby boomers, they are saving only about one-third of what they will need to maintain their current standard of living during retirement.[5] In a recent study by

Allstate Financial Corporation, participants reported having an average of only $120,000 in retirement savings; yet it is projected that these boomers will need $1 million to cover living expenses without depending on Social Security.[6]

Workplace change can be pretty scary when you are mortgaged to the hilt and your employer announces yet another downsizing.

We were comfortable in our jobs. In a hierarchical industrial-era workplace, the boss made the decisions and we simply followed orders. If you were a "good soldier," you expected to be set until you decided to retire to that little retirement village in Florida. Ah, life was good for the "mainstream" boomer. And then change came—not just little change, but big change. Whole industries were eliminated or subsumed. New and very different skills were required, from computer literacy to meeting facilitation.

It all seemed to happen so fast that we did not know what hit us. But we did know that we were losing our jobs, being asked to perform in ways that were foreign to us, asked to do more with fewer resources, and told our companies were being merged, sold, or reorganized — again!

Needless to say, employees reacted. Workers continue to report declining levels of satisfaction. Boomers are the least satisfied. In fact, boomers report a decline in job satisfaction from 57 percent to 47 percent over a five-year period at the end of the '90s, according to an April 2001 survey conducted by the Conference Board, a worldwide network of business executives.[7] Boomers are not satisfied with pay increases and benefits because raises have been fewer and benefits have decreased. Real income increased 11 percent between 1970 and 1975, and only two percent between 1990 and 1995.[8] In medium and large companies, 92 percent of the employees had medical insurance in 1989.[9] By 1997, only 76 percent had coverage.[10] The changes are real, pervasive, and almost unbearable for some boomers.

How do we know that boomers are not coping well?

Workplace violence — second only to highway crashes as the cause of work-related deaths — is a major concern for corporate America.[11] Pinkerton's annual security survey of Fortune 1000 companies indicates that workplace violence was the number one concern for America's largest corporations' security managers in 2001.[12] Reports are splashed across our television and computer screens every day with news of yet more incidents of workplace violence. There's even a new name—"desk rage"—for more subtle forms of violence. These are the increasingly common emotional outbursts, expressions of rudeness, and physical attacks on technological devices. Boomers are working longer hours than ever before, and women and men struggle to balance home and career.

There is no doubt that the pain of change is taking its toll. What can we do to cope when there is literally no end in sight?

I believe that baby boomers and everyone in the workplace can adapt to change. We just need to reframe our view of the world and where we fit in it. It is an individual journey, not a team exercise. Who you can become—the value you can offer in this new workplace—is up to you. This book is about finding your "authentic self" in the midst of the clutter and noise that is around you. All of the "records" in your head that say, "This is the way I have to be and this is what I have to do to successfully earn a living," need to be broken.

> *Change yourself and your work will seem different.*
>
> *Norman Vincent Peale,*
> *20th-Century Minister and American Author*

It is a new day, especially for us baby boomers who may be nearing the end of one career, but need or want to continue to contribute positively to the economy. If you are 50, you could conceivably have another 20 years to be gainfully productive.

We think so much is out of our control in the workplace today, but it really isn't. This is one of the "records" that we need to break. Everything you need to succeed is within your reach because it is within you.

This is not a book about the technical competencies that you might need, even though different skill sets are required for success in the new work world. It is about reconnecting to your inner source of power to help you rediscover your true calling and unique gifts that you can offer the workplace and the universe.

I wrote this book because, as a consultant, I have interviewed over 9,000 people in corporate America in the last 10 years and the message is pretty much the same from all of them: "My spirit is broken." We can't give our best selves with broken spirits. The economy needs everyone with all that we have to give. But, more importantly, we owe it to ourselves to find our kernel of genius — our unique gift.

My life journey has taught me that we have more power than we think, more choices than we imagine. When we are willing to unleash our potential, new energies and capabilities spill forth. In listening to workers' concerns, I often see my own insecurities and fear of the unknown. I wrote this book to help the millions of baby boomers and other workers who feel like victims with no alternative to an unhappy work environment and an uncertain future.

This book cannot predict where your future lies. But it can help you explore new ways of looking at your life and work. So, whether you are struggling to find peace and self-fulfillment in your present position, searching for a new job or livelihood, or thinking about joining the ranks of the self-employed, *this book is for you.*

Rapid change will outlast our lifetimes. We need not only to get used to it but to learn to be at peace with it. But we may never like it. Probably, it really is, "only wet babies who like change." Because like babies, we all want to feel comfortable and secure. And we can have security and peace of mind only if we realize that it is not going to come from some outside source. It's within.

This book is intended to help you reframe your concept of work, embrace change with new vigor, or at least learn new coping skills, and unleash dormant potential within.

It is a book about finding you—the authentic you in all of your splendor with rare and precious gifts yet untapped.

To help you on the journey, each chapter ends with a summary of key points, reflective questions, and an affirmation. What is an affirmation? It is a statement of belief—belief in yourself. It is an intention. It is a declaration and promise to yourself to seek your truest essence, your highest self.

> *Work like you don't need the money, love like you have never been hurt and dance as if no one is watching.*
>
> *Anonymous*

Chapter 1
Setting the Context Part I:
Baby Boomers, Smug and Secure

But let's not kid ourselves, overall we've had it pretty good. We've made our mark. We began our lives as the indulged 'little emperors and empresses' of our households. We emerged from our protected neighborhoods intensely idealistic and so ill-disciplined we expected social changes to come as easily as ordering from an F.A.O. Schwartz catalogue.

Howard Smead, Contemporary American Historian,
University of Maryland, and Author, from
Don't Trust Anyone Over Thirty: A History of the Baby Boom

This book is intended to prepare you for, and guide you through, an important journey—a journey of rethinking your work life, and in so doing, rethinking your life—rethinking you. Before you can really begin the journey, you need to understand how you got to where you are now—the context that has shaped your attitudes, values, principles, opinions, and your very being.

We sometimes underestimate the role our past has in shaping our present and our future. By understanding the path that has gotten many of us to where we are today, we can better begin to "unlearn" some of our assumptions, values, and beliefs, which simply do not hold true in today's workplace.

Being a Boomer

If you are one of almost 80 million people living in the United States today who were born between 1946 and 1964, your mindset has been deeply shaped by the baby boom phenomenon.[1] The virtual explosion of births following World War II created a distinct segment of the population, representing 28 percent of all Americans.[2] According to the 2000 census, 63 million are white, nine million are African American, eight million are Hispanic or Latino, and about four million are Asian, Native American, and Alaska Native. We are almost 50 percent men and 50 percent women.[3]

In 2002, we, the baby boomers, are between the ages of 38 and 56. Those of us at the older end of the age spectrum entered the workplace during the heyday of the post-World War II industrial expansion, the era of entitlement and job security. We thought we could find our niche, work hard, be loyal to one company and, in exchange, we would be set for life — regular salary increases, good benefits, upward mobility, and a great retirement package.

We were told that we could live better than the previous generation. Our parents drilled into our heads that they wanted us to fare better from a socioeconomic standpoint than they did.

Especially for African Americans and other disenfranchised groups, the industrial expansion after World War II opened doors that had not just been closed but locked with no key. Millions of immigrants and blacks from the South came to the North and northeastern United States to find their "pot of gold." They got jobs in factories that could not produce goods and services fast enough to keep up with demand for steel, rubber, and chemicals to make "better mouse traps" to satisfy what seemed to be an insatiable demand for consumer products, from gadgets to cars. Life was good, or at least better. It was still harder for minorities, who got the lowest paying jobs and were the last hired and first fired. Women essentially stopped working after World War II and gave the factory jobs back to men. Women would not play a key role in the industrial-era workplace until the early '70s.

Despite the issues for segments who were not invited to participate fully in the industrial era, a new standard of living was set and the bar kept being raised as the years from 1900 moved us through World War I, the Great Depression, and then World War II. It was after World War II that the factories rebounded, hired millions of people, and spurred the next phase of the industrial era.

While war veterans filled jobs in myriad manufacturing concerns, women went home to have babies. From 1946 to 1964, almost 80 million people were born — more than any time before or since in our history. The term "baby boomers" is used to identify this unique population cohort.

Baby boomers' belief and value system is based on the fundamental promise of a better life than the previous generation. Even for disenfranchised groups, for the first time, there was hope. Baby boomers did not experience the Great Depression like many of their parents. They grew up in expanding economic times when the idea of this better life was not just a "pipe dream." Our parents told us that we could have it better than they did. We needed to get an education, find a good job ("good" meant as much money as you could get, but not necessarily a job you liked), and settle down (get married, have two children, and stay with one employer until you retired).

The picture of success for the typical baby boomer was painted with material acquisitions, always just a little bit better, a little bit bigger than the neighbors ("keepin' up with the Joneses"), credit cards charged to the maximum, and mortgages on suburban homes stretched to the limits of the banker's imagination. Bottom line: Baby boomers value money. The more you have (or have access to), the more successful you are perceived to be.

The desire to earn and spend as much money as possible is inextricably linked to job stability. It is only with job security that we can spend money that we don't have today but have a high assurance we will have in the future. Job security afforded baby boomers a certain freedom and "smugness" up through the '70s.

The Civil Rights Movement and the Women's Liberation Movement of the '60s opened doors for women and minorities in the workforce in the early '70s. The almighty two-income family became the rule rather than the exception. We could spend even more money!

We could pay for more "toys" on time, charge them, or put them on layaway. You could have whatever you wanted, when you wanted it, because you would always have a paycheck each week to keep pace with the "time payments." Even if you did not have a college degree, a blue-collar job afforded you the opportunity to amass material goods like no other generation.

Previous generations had a strong saving ethic that we did not think was necessary any more. After all, we had Social Security and a lucrative retirement plan. We were set for life.

We didn't think we needed to save as our parents did.

According to a study done by the American Association of Retired Persons (AARP), compared to previous generations, baby boomers say they need more money than their parents to live comfortably and are more self-indulgent than their parents.[4]

We, baby boomers, are known for our "make-it, spend-it" mentality: "If I'm making good money, I should be able to spend it on whatever makes me happy." Boomers are the ultimate consumers, and proud of it.

After all, we work hard. We are entitled to have what we want.

Our smug, entitlement values worked as long as there was job security, but, as we all know too well, the grand industrial era—with all of its boom and fanfare—began to crumble as technology started on an acceleration curve that nobody could have predicted. Automation got a jump-start in the late '70s, and technological advances kept coming faster and faster, causing a complete metamorphosis of the economy and workplace. They are still coming so fast that many of us can't even see the changes coming until they hit us. For many baby boomers, the transformation to the New Economy has knocked us down and we haven't been able to get back up again.

> *The old economy centered on big manufacturers, surrounded by small local service businesses...giant auto makers and mom and pop dealerships and repair shops. In the emerging economy, it is the reverse. At the core will be big knowledge brokers, drawing on global pools of information and insight. They'll be surrounded by small firms producing highly specialized goods, components and services that can be assembled and packaged practically anywhere.*
>
> *Robert Reich, Former Secretary of Labor under William Clinton, 42nd President of the United States*

Let's take a brief look at what has happened and some of the interrelated manifestations of the workplace.

Global Competition:

United States companies were very arrogant about their market dominance up through the mid-'70s. I worked for a Fortune 100 company that enjoyed an 80 percent market share. Over the last 30 years, due to formidable global competition, it has seen that share erode substantially. You can name just about any industry — automobile, copier, photographic, computer, other consumer electronics, and financial. None have been spared. The widely held assumption that we can "build a better mousetrap" and the world would come "running to our door" was shattered. Consumers now had new choices and began to exercise them. In 1970, 13 percent of new automobiles purchased in the US were imports. In 1987, that number had more than doubled.[5]

The company I worked for argued vehemently in 1979 that its customers were loyal and would not buy Japanese products. This is the same company that is struggling today. It is the same company that is trying desperately to change employee mindsets, to help them understand that the days of yore with big bonuses, healthy raises, and complete benefits packages are but fleeting memories. It is the same company that is trying to help employees understand that "all bets are off" and "fairness" is a moving target with today's volatile business conditions. It is the same company that wants employees to step up and be responsible for their own futures.

I know that this company is not unique. There are hundreds of American corporations that were complacent—even arrogant—during their heydays of the good times during the industrial era.

But baby boomers are a stubborn lot and are trying desperately to hang onto the "rules" of the good ole' days. Many blame the leadership of their companies and cannot accept that the transformation has little to do with management skills and everything to do with a fundamental shift from the industrial to the knowledge era. The key to this shift is rapidly advancing technology.

Technology:

Who could have predicted the impact of a little electronic chip when it was developed in the mid-'40s? The miniaturization of the chip has resulted in the ability to improve existing products and create new ones at lightning speed, which transforms the way we live and work on a daily basis. Automation is the reason for the shift from a manufacturing to a service economy.

Technology results in easier entry for competition. New businesses that start in garages and dorm rooms are displacing traditional companies as attractive investments. Previously, companies that invented new technology had a two-to-three-year jump on the competition; now maybe they have a six-month advantage before somebody creates a similar or substitute product that does the same thing faster and better.

> *Once a new technology rolls over you, if you're not part of the steamroller, you're part of the road.*
>
> Stewart Brand, 20th-Century American Physics Professor
> at the University of Durham, Durham, England

We still don't fully understand the impact of the Internet on our lives. It is safe to say, though, that it is in the process of not only transforming how we communicate but how we shop, how we conduct research, even how we read books. I predict that libraries as we know them today will be extinct within the next 10 years. There will be no reason to leave home to access any resource that one might want.

For the most part, baby boomers have embraced technology, with more of us owning home computers than pre-boomers or Generation Xers (GenXers, a term used for individuals born between 1965 and 1981, or some say as early as 1961). Still it scares us because of the rapidity of the rate of change and the increased expectations in the workplace to keep up. Just when you think you have learned a particular software, a new version comes along and you have to learn it all over again. It surely can be a stress inducer.

> *Technology is a gift from God. After the gift of life, it is perhaps the greatest of God's gifts. It is the mother of civilizations, of arts and of sciences.*
>
> *Freeman John Dyson, Contemporary English Writer, Physicist, and Educator*

Skill Requirements:

The industrial era needed brawn. The New Economy, or knowledge era, needs brain. Gone are the days of repetitive, routine tasks, directed by rigid standard operating procedures (SOPs). I remember jobs where my role was to develop these SOPs — rules that were to be followed, point for point, to accomplish various outcomes. The purpose was to reduce the variability in approach, thus reducing error. This model worked as long as the system remained stable, but that is clearly not the case anymore.

> *Globalization has changed us into a company that searches the world, not just to sell or source, but to find intellectual capital ... the world's best talents and greatest ideas.*
>
> Jack Welch, *Former CEO, General Electric Company*

The total quality management movement of the early '80s taught us that continuous improvement was the new order of the day. It also taught us that good ideas were not confined to the management ranks. Everybody needed to be a part of the process of continually improving processes, procedures, and practices in order to keep up with competition. These ideas led to such concepts as quality circles, participatory management, self-directed work teams, and empowerment.

My research tells me that many baby boomers rejected these new ideas. I have heard time and time again in employee focus groups objections such as the following:

"I am not being paid the big bucks like the managers. Let them make the decisions."

"I just want to be left alone to do my job. I am not interested in participating."

"Just tell me what you want me to do."

Some baby boomers can't seem to shake the old dictum of "leave your brain at the door," which was how it was in the industrial era. How many times did we hear, "You are not being paid to think"? When I went into industry in the mid-'70s, I was college educated and hired for a management-trainee position, but I still got a strong message of,

"Just do as you are told. We really don't want your ideas."

Today, your ideas measure your value. In interviews with executives, they readily agree that they can train people to perform the tasks related to a job—what they need are people who are creative, willing to experiment, "think outside the box," take risks and, in essence, be pioneers. The "just let me do my job" mindset is dead and can be deadly to your career.

> *Continuing to cling to patterns you know inhibits your ability to discover what you don't know.*
>
> *Eric Allenbaugh, Contemporary Business Consultant, Executive Coach, and Author*

Baby boomers must own up to the reality that being the best engineer or the smartest laboratory technician is not enough anymore. You also have to be a great facilitator, communicator, "networker" and relationship builder, just to name a few of the knowledge-era skills that add value to a company's bottom line.

New Economy Companies:

Traditional companies that have their roots in the industrial era have been dubbed as "dinosaurs." They are having difficulty keeping up with the fast pace of the New Economy. They are big, overly bureaucratic, hold steadfast to a hierarchical structure, and unwittingly foster an entitlement mentality in employees.

The trend is toward small, nimble companies that have virtually no hierarchy, reward people for results, and consistently reinvent themselves. These high-risk companies know that there are no guarantees; and just as many as are started, are stopped abruptly because they could not make it. The rash of dot-com companies that have come and gone during 2000 to 2001 is a case in point.

New Economy employees understand that there can be no guarantees for long-term employment. They take the risk, which can lead to huge rewards or nothing. There is no middle ground.

Future opportunities will not be with the "dinosaurs" but with organizations that can change with the speed of need. But as we see today, the risk is high, and only a few of the best of the new breed of companies are making it. Translation: No job security for anybody.

As baby boomers nearing traditional retirement age, some of you may contemplate a second career or starting your own business. There are clearly limitless opportunities today, but only if you can transform your thinking about what work is, redefine "job," and truly understand the notion of constant "reinvention."

The New Economy affords us a real chance to follow our dreams. This idea may sound like a hackneyed cliché, but pursuing your passion is probably more possible today than it ever has been. Technology has reduced, or even eliminated, barriers to easily starting your own business. When we were counseled by our parents, most of us were advised to "get a good job and settle down." Nobody told me to follow my dreams or to pursue my passion and the money would follow. They said, "Go for the money!"

17

> *You may lose your job tomorrow, maybe this after-noon. Or you may have to close an entire division. This is the price for being in the most dynamic part of the New Economy, doing creative stuff, taking big risks. It goes with the territory.*
>
> Robert Reich

As a first generation college graduate of a laborer father and a homemaker mother, I was told to get a job that paid as much as possible. Nobody really cared if I liked it. As a matter of fact, when I complained some years before I left corporate America that I was not fulfilled, some thought I needed therapy. They said, "What is wrong with her? She has a good job—one not open to African Americans just 10 years ago. How can she complain? She is doing so much better than many of us."

If I am typical, then many of you may also have been in careers that were not necessarily what you believed you were "called" to do while on this earth. As a matter of fact, an April 2001 survey by the Conference Board showed that baby boomers registered the lowest level of job satisfaction among all workers.[6]

The New Economy, with all of its chaos, instability, and craziness, has led to disturbing trends like "desk rage" and workplace violence. Even though these phenomena are disturbing, it suggests that people are having personal, emotional reactions to the transforming workplace. If you turn this around to the positive, it can lead you to really take stock of yourself and what you truly want to do.

I was so miserable in corporate America that I went home in tears every night. I felt stifled and unfulfilled. While I had to experience a great deal of pain and emotional upheaval, it forced me to look deep within for the answers. I did not use management or discrimination as scapegoats, even though both were factors.

> **It is what you do with your life that counts.**
> *Martin Luther King, Jr., 20th-Century Civil Rights Activist*

I finally decided to take the risk of leaving and starting my own business. That was 18 years ago and while there have been life-altering challenges, I have been able to pursue what I feel called to do.

The contrasts between the industrial age and the New Economy are stark, as shown in Figure 1. The metamorphosis is as great as when we transitioned from the agricultural to the industrial era. We are in the throes of a total upheaval of the social order.

Figure 1

Industrial Age Business	*The New Economy*
Mass market productivity	Customized products and services
Labor-intensive	Mind-intensive
"Things"	Knowledge
Manual processes	Technology-driven processes
Bigger is better	Better is better
Lowest cost	Value-added
Standard operating procedures	Flexibility and adaptability
Inventory-laden	Just-in-time
Domestic	Global
Homogeneity	Diversity
Several related services	Micro-specialized core competency
Mega business	Small cottage industries
Employees Free agents	Entitlement Self-sufficiency
Hierarchical	Self-directed
Management	Leadership
Stability	Change

> *Science and technology revolutionize our lives, but memory, tradition and myth frame our response. Expelled from individual consciousness by the rush of change, history finds its revenge by stamping the collective unconsciousness with habits, values, expectations, dreams. The dialectic between past and future will continue to form our lives.*
>
> Arthur M. Schlesinger, Jr.,
> *Contemporary American Historian, Author,*
> *and Special Assistant to John F. Kennedy,*
> *35th President of the United States*

What does this mean for you?

It means that more than ever, you need to truly know who you are and what you stand for. It means that you have to be firmly grounded in the core values that guide your life. With all of the change around you, it will swallow you up in chaos and confusion, even to the point of dysfunction if you lack a deep understanding of self. When you have a deep understanding of self, you are more able to reconcile the conflict that arises when the impending change is not in sync with your current values and beliefs. You cannot hope to survive and, ultimately, thrive in transition if you are not willing to make personal changes. It is hard to even contemplate personal change when you don't know your current self.

The New Economy requires a whole new mindset for everyone, especially us baby boomers. The dependence on an employer for our sense of security and well being is a well-entrenched expectation. We must totally shift our assumptions and turn the responsibility from an external to an internal locus of control. Your destiny is controlled by you, not others.

There is already a new breed cropping up all over the workforce that knows how to do just that—the GenXers. When you first encountered them in the workplace, you may have thought that they were the ones who just didn't get it. They job hop. They expect to "have a say" in everything. They demand flexibility. They don't respect the 9-to-5 parameters of the workday. They are obsessed with increasing their own skill portfolio, and they act like they were born with computers at their fingertips and cell phones attached to their ears. When the dot-com economy collapsed in 2001, the GenXers who lost their jobs had an entirely different attitude than a baby boomer would have. They are a career-resilient bunch and easily transitioned into other pursuits. They decided to go back to school, to look for work in an entirely new field, to start their own businesses, or to relocate to be closer to family.

> *I don't believe in circumstances. The people who get on in this world are the people who get up and look for circumstances they want.*
>
> George Bernard Shaw, 20th-Century British Playwright

Interestingly, today they embody just what employers want in job candidates. An emerging new breed of employers needs workers who value learning and mentoring more than longevity and career path. Today's employers want people who are not afraid to voice their diverse opinions and who are a step ahead of the curve—whether it is in providing good service or acquiring new skills. They don't need workers chained to their desks for eight hours a day—they need people ready to work whenever deadlines need to be met, from wherever they can best get the job done.

Baby boomers can learn a lot from their young counterparts. It is a whole new mindset.

Anything But Ready to Retire

Are you thinking, "Why do I have to bother? I don't want to learn a whole new way to work or live my life. Not at my age."

Think again.

Every nine seconds, another baby boomer turns 50. According to a survey sponsored by the Del Webb Corporation, many baby boomers are keenly aware that work is still a big part of their futures. More than half even expect that part-time work will be a hallmark of baby boomer "retirement." Predictions are that baby boomers are seven times more likely than previous generations to start a new career in "retirement." And most boomers surveyed say that they do not expect to have enough money to retire at age 55.[7] According to an AARP study, 17 percent of baby boomers say they expect to start their own businesses.[8]

So work—and finding personal fulfillment in work—is more important than ever before for baby boomers. While it is bad enough to feel frustrated and confused now, you don't want to spend your "golden years" trapped in a job or career that leaves you unhappy. Now is the time to take charge.

> *If you want to succeed you should strike out on new paths rather than travel the worn paths of accepted success.*
>
> John D. Rockefeller, 20th-Century Industrialist, Philanthropist, and CEO of Standard Oil Company

Create Your Own Context

Whether you have already been downsized, worry every day that you may get caught in the next round of cuts, or are just ready to look at work and your future in a whole new light, you are the only one who can design your destiny. My personal journey has taught me that we have more power than we think, more choices than we imagine.

Today's success requires innovation, technological savvy, the shedding of narrow descriptions of functions, global thinking, new ways of problem-solving, and a relentless questioning of why and how to do "it" better. Success also includes caring and compassion, empathy and integrity, respect for diversity, the acceptance of ambiguity, uncertainty and paradoxes, a positive outlook, a hopeful spirit, and a high level of self-awareness.

You can create your own context. "What has my experience been? How has it prepared me or ill-prepared me for the New Economy? What do I need to learn? And unlearn? What do I know about myself? What is it I have always wanted to do—felt called to do? How can I find real meaning in my life? How can I create my very own "brand"—the unique, the authentic me?"

> *Sometimes you've got to let everything go — purge yourself. If you are unhappy with anything... whatever is bringing you down, get rid of it. Because you'll find that when you're free, your true creativity, your true self comes out.*
>
> Tina Turner, Contemporary American
> Rhythm-and-Blues Singer

The good news is that everything you need to re-create yourself to thrive in the New Economy is already within you. Many baby boomers have spent their lives conforming and adapting to others' expectations. The years have given us a depth of understanding (wisdom) that GenXers don't have yet. If we combine our wisdom with their mindsets about work, we will truly be awesome. We will realize that finding oneself and pursuing only that which gives us the greatest joy will lead to peace, self-fulfillment, and prosperity.

> *Nothing outside yourself can save you; nothing outside yourself can give you peace.*
>
> From A Course in Miracles, Foundation for Inner Peace

Affirmation: I understand the context in which I formed my attitudes about work, and I can create a whole new context for myself. I will take responsibility for my own employability and my own self-fulfillment. I have all that I need within.

Summary of Key Points:

- Being part of the baby boom generation has made a significant impact on our value system and the way most of us view employment, the workplace, and money.

- We are in the midst of a monumental transformation from the industrial age to the New Economy, each marked by two completely different sets of principles.

- The knowledge era rocked our world, requiring us to rethink how we view work and ourselves, today and in the future.

- Generation X has not only adapted but is creating the model for what employers are looking for in workers.

- Full retirement anytime soon is probably not an option, but coming closer to traditional retirement age is one more reason to rethink your own employability and views of work.

- You can create a new context for yourself. You have all you need inside yourself.

Ask Yourself:

1. When I started my career, what did I expect from my employer? What did I take for granted, based on past experience or expectations?

2. What do I need to really be comfortable? To be confident my family is provided for?

3. What are my attitudes about money and how do they influence what I do and do not do?

4. When did I first realize my career may not go as I had planned?

5. How have I responded? What have I done? Not done?

6. Have I encountered GenXers at work who embody these new principles? What do I think of them?

7. Do I expect to retire sometime soon? Is that realistic?

8. Do I really like what I do? Is there something else I've always wanted to do? Why haven't I done it?

9. Do I know that I have all that I need inside myself to reinvent my future?

Chapter 2

Setting the Context Part II: "For the Love of Money"

If a person gets his attitude about money straight, it will straighten out almost every other area of his life.

Billy Graham, Contemporary American Evangelist

Baby boomers changed the entire value system of this country. For one, we turned our focus from such values as character, integrity, and compassion and started to equate success with the size of one's bank account.

When I grew up in the '60s, the most respected workers were teachers, preachers, and undertakers.

The teacher nurtured the children and inspired them to dream bigger dreams.

The preacher knew from the depths of his being the trials and tribulations African Americans faced as a people on a daily basis. Every Sunday, he connected to our souls, lifted our spirits, and fueled us with just enough hope to make it through another week.

When we died prematurely from broken spirits, shattered dreams, and weary hearts, the black funeral director was there with a special kind of comfort and caring for the survivors.

Many young black women coming of age in the '60s aspired to the teaching profession—one of the few careers open to us. If your son or brother got the calling to preach, mothers and sisters joined the rest of the community shouting praises to Jesus. Only a few were fortunate enough to be born into the funeral director's family. It went without saying that a funeral director's son would carry on the family business.

When I grew up in the '60s, my role models were not millionaires. Money did not make people special at that time. They were special because of their character, integrity, and the difference they made in the community.

Today, crises abound in the fields of teaching and preaching. A National Center for Education Statistics study predicts that we will need 2.4 million new teachers in classrooms by 2008.[1] At the same time, a Bureau of Labor Statistics report predicts that 796,000 baby boom generation elementary and secondary teachers will retire between 1998 and 2008.[2]

And despite teaching having once been such a respected profession among African Americans, the National Center for Education Statistics reports that today 42 percent of U.S. public schools have no teachers of color, even though students of color comprise one-third of enrollment. It is expected that the number of teachers of color will fall even lower, making up only five percent of the teaching workforce.[3]

Relative to the ministry, a study of mainline churches conducted by the Louisville Institute in Kentucky revealed that there had been a sharp drop in the numbers of young ordained clergy in the last 25 years. In the mid-'70s, ordained clergy 35 years old and under represented 20 percent to 25 percent of the total ordained clergy, while in 2000, they represented only four to eight percent.[4]

According to a U.S. Conference of Catholic Bishops study in 2000, the number of priests available for pastoral ministry has not kept up with church growth. Today, 82 percent of dioceses report that they don't have enough priests to meet their pastoral needs.[5]

This decline is not, however, carrying over to as many African-American churches. Ongoing respect for the ministry in the community, mentoring, innovative approaches that appeal to youth, and the fact that women are being encouraged to become ministers have all contributed to maintaining and growing a healthy number of clergy in African-American churches.

Even so, teaching and preaching are no longer preferred professions or vocations for most young people, no matter what their race or gender. Large corporations have bought many black-owned funeral homes because the funeral directors' sons or daughters are no longer interested in taking over the family business.

Social Upheaval

It seems as if our value system shifted abruptly in the mid- to late-'70s when suddenly our success was measured by how much money we made, not necessarily by the content of our characters.

The affirmative action movement of the '70s opened doors to professions previously barred to women and people of color. Before that, a college-educated black person had almost no chance of getting a professional job in business. White women and women of color from affluent families who went to college often did so to find a husband; it really did not matter what field they studied. They would work only a few years, if at all, until they started a family.

I came from a lower-income family during the heyday of affirmative action. I was the first person in my family to go to college. My parents strongly encouraged me to go into teaching and thought I was crazy for thinking there was any other option. When I went to college, I did not know what I wanted to do, but I knew teaching was not my personal calling. I saw glimpses of new possibilities for someone who looked like me, and I wanted to explore them all.

Still, my goal was not necessarily to make a lot of money, but rather to be able to support myself comfortably. My mother drilled into my head not to rely on a man for support. In her mind, teaching was a sure bet. How could she think otherwise? The only "successful" black women she knew were teachers.

When I entered college in 1969, all of America was going through a social and political transformation on the magnitude of today's New Economy metamorphosis, and boomers were at the center of it all. The Civil Rights Movement was at its peak. The Women's Liberation Movement was being spawned. The country was "in conflict" with Vietnam. And our long-held ideologies about sex were being challenged. "Free love" and "make love, not war" were the mantras of the day.

We were experiencing a total upheaval of the social order, and our world would never be the same again. Baby boomers challenged every conceivable injustice of modern America during the '60s and '70s: voting rights, segregation laws, women's rights, abortion laws, and defense policies. It was an era of monumental change.

The oldest baby boomer was 23 in 1969, and the youngest was five. The lesson we learned and preached: You don't have to accept the status quo. Stand up and fight for what you believe. You are an American entitled to equality and justice, by whatever means necessary.

During my undergraduate years, we protested for some cause every weekend. It was Kent State, Jackson State, the Vietnam War, the low number of students of color admitted by universities, and others. We called for the dismissal of a professor who, we thought, had made a racial slur. We held the university president hostage in the faculty club. We staged "sit-ins" in the cafeteria and painted the huge rock located outside one of the largest dorms black to call attention to "black power."

It was an era of activism, awakening, and the colliding of two worlds—the old model with egalitarian ideals. In the new vision, everyone was entitled to enjoy the fruits of prosperity, no matter what color, creed, or gender.

The '70s opened new opportunities. Segregated organizations from corporate America to private country clubs were forced to make room for blacks, women, Hispanics, Asians, and the disabled. Businesses, education, and government were required to show good-faith efforts at integrating their ranks. The requirement to hire and promote women and people of color was enacted into law with the Civil Rights Act of 1964 and subsequent Executive Orders.

> *We have talked long enough in this country about equal rights...it is time now to write the next chapter...and to write it in the book of laws.*
>
> Lyndon Baines Johnson, 36th President of the United States

The combination of a growing demand for consumer goods and services and affirmative action efforts changed the financial prospects for the majority of the baby boom generation. It is reported that five million minority members and six million white women and women of color have benefited from affirmative action.[6] Clearly, the "pot of gold" was no longer the sole domain of the white male. Affirmative action forced organizations to be much more deliberate about their hiring practices.

At the same time, organizations definitely ensured that white men would not lose out due to affirmative action, so the "pie" was enlarged and the "bar" was raised. To maintain the differential in status between white men and women and people of color, white men were simply given larger raises and bigger titles. Profits were growing. Organizations could afford a "little fat" in the payroll. And the affirmative action hires were not always given meaningful work or opportunities to grow even though their titles may have been impressive.

Even though they were still lagging behind white males,

people of color and women were better off financially than they were before. On the surface, it seemed that everyone was happy. Median weekly salaries increased by about 53 percent between 1985 and 1998. It is interesting to note, however, that in 1985, women's and African Americans' salaries were on average 54 percent lower than white men's salaries. By 1998, the gap narrowed, but women still lagged behind men by 31 percent and African Americans lagged by 40 percent.[7]

As is the case with any inequitable system, this could not sustain itself forever. People of color and women wanted to progress through the ranks like their white male counterparts. So as the "bar" continued to be raised, salaries in businesses started to outpace those in government and education by wide margins. Government and education are bound by laws and regulations that prevent them from playing the money game to the extent that the free enterprise system can. In 1962, schoolteachers, government workers and federal employees were paid comparable salaries. In fact, teachers made slightly more than the others. Since

1994, however, salary offers for college graduates in all fields have grown at twice the rate as those for new teachers. In 1999, new college graduates received average salary offers in excess of $37,000 compared to an average beginning teacher's salary of $26,639. Today's average teacher salary represents an increase of only $135 (or 70 cents a day) in constant dollars over the average salary in 1972 to 1973.[8]

By the late 1970s, money was clearly the standard measurement of how well you were faring in the world. We could see people's success by where they lived, how they dressed, and the kind of car they drove. In essence, money was synonymous with success. Almost everyone's goal was to find the career that was going to pay the most money. The majority of those jobs were in corporate America, so we advised our children, nieces, nephews, and cousins to prepare for a job in business. In 1970, there were just 26,000 master's degrees awarded in business management/administrative services. That number doubled by 1980 and rose another 74 percent to 94,000 by 1995.[9]

> *We've only been wealthy in this country for 70 years.*
> *Who said we ought to have all this? Is it ordained?*
>
> Jack Welch

Business was definitely the career of choice because that is where the big bucks were, and money and success went hand in hand. No longer did we perceive social service, education, or other helping professions as laudable pursuits.

Did baby boomers sell out? Whatever happened to the idealism of the '60s — the social justice causes for which we fought so hard? According to Howard Smead, we have shifted from liberalism to conservatism: "In 1975, 46 percent of those boomers old enough to be surveyed called themselves liberal. Ten years later, that percentage fell 29 percent. Now it's below 20 percent."[10]

We were living the fruits of our labors! We had fought a good fight and now we were entitled to relax a little and enjoy our efforts. After all, the whole idea was to make a better world for all, and hadn't we done that?

People of color have never been totally comfortable with the idea of resting on our laurels. We are expected to reach back to help those coming behind us and those who went before us, who have not fared so well. As a matter of fact, "successful" people of color are subject to sharp criticism by the new breed of civil rights leaders for moving to the suburbs and "forgetting" the masses who have not "moved on up." Even though more of us have been able to gain financial success, the economic inequities are getting bigger, not smaller, in some arenas. But it doesn't stop individuals in any socio-economic station from trying to get "theirs."

> *Whatever affects one directly, affects all indirectly. I can never be what I ought to be until you are what you ought to be. This is the interrelated structure of reality.*
>
> *Martin Luther King, Jr.*

The Meaning of Money

Our society has become so driven by money as the status symbol of success that whether or not it is obtained by legal and ethical means is sometimes secondary. We can point to countless situations in America where financial gain and greed have been at the root of the behavior. Huge scandals like Michael Milken's violation of federal securities and racketeering laws caught our attention in the late '80s. Milken, an American financial executive at Drexel Burnham Lambert, Inc., known as the "junk bond king," was paid $846 million by Drexel and was later sentenced to prison for his actions.[11]

White-collar crime continues at an all-time high, spanning high-powered executives to support staff workers and consumers. The 2002 scandal at Enron, a previously highly regarded, fast growing energy trading company where executives were investigated for misrepresenting financial performance, is but another example.

Insurance fraud is a $95-billion-a-year scam.[12] Credit card fraud costs taxpayers nearly $3 billion annually.[13]

John Bennett, the head of New Era Philanthropy, was behind America's biggest charity scam. Over $135 million was swindled from hundreds of charities, universities, and nonprofit organizations. In 1997, Bennett was brought up on 82 counts of money laundering, fraud, and tax violations.[14] This is not an isolated case. More than $21 billion is stolen from charities each year, as reported by Louis Mizell, Jr., in his book, *Masters of Deception.*[15]

Sadly, the heroes in many urban communities today are drug dealers. Why? Because they make a lot of money and own expensive sports cars, jewelry, and clothes.

Americans, with baby boomers leading the pack, have become totally obsessed with "getting rich." One of the most popular publishing topics today is how to become wealthy. Books like *The Millionaire Next Door* and *The Millionaire Mind* by Thomas J. Stanley, Ph.D., are best sellers.

> *Money is the most important thing in the world. It represents health, strength, honor, generosity, and beauty as conspicuously as the want of it represents illness, weakness, disgrace, meanness and ugliness.*
>
> George Bernard Shaw

And as we get older, we are even more interested in how to get rich without working hard. The number of "get-rich-quick" gurus plastered on our television screens and advertising on the Internet is growing daily.

With stable jobs in growing companies, many baby boomers were able to live very comfortably, continually moving up the economic ladder of success. As long as there was little risk of losing your job, you could project earnings into the future and purchase to the risk limit that was personally comfortable for you. And that is what we did. As advertising methods became more sophisticated, we were lured into buying whatever it was that was going to make us more beautiful, give us more leisure time, or put brighter smiles on our faces.

Buy, buy, buy! Spend, spend, spend! It became a vicious cycle. Lower income people watched the same advertisements as high-income people. They, too, wanted the same brighter smiles. The "spend-it-all" mentality knows no specific socioeconomic group, no specific color, or gender. Many Americans spend all that they make and more. Consumer debt is out of control. In December 2001, U.S. consumers had $1.7 trillion in debt, twice that of a decade before, when there was $800 billion in debt.[16] People of all socioeconomic groups buy, beg, borrow, and sometimes even steal so they can acquire material accoutrements.

The two-income household phenomenon has created the illusion that we can spend even more. When employment doors opened for women in the early '70s, this new social fact of life was born. We began to trade off leisure time and quality family time to work as many hours as possible so that we could be as successful as possible. When I had children in the late '70s and wrestled with whether I was going to stay home or work, I succumbed to the argument that it is not the quantity but the quality of time you spend with your children that counts. I had to advance in my career so that I could make enough to pay for child-care, a house-keeper, and other personal services, which I no longer had time to perform myself. Yes, I had a supportive husband; but he, too, was busy doing what he needed to do to climb the corporate ladder. Again, it was a vicious cycle. The more you make, the more you spend, and the more you need to make.

We convinced ourselves that an inflationary economy was the reason that both parents had to work. Based on changes in the consumer price index, inflation in 1960 was 1.4 percent. It rose to 5.6 percent by 1970, then to 12.5 percent by 1980, but dropped to 6.1 percent by 1990.[17] By then, we could no longer make ends meet with just one income. We convinced ourselves that it had nothing to do with our financial expectations or our desire to give our children every material item that we never had. It had nothing to do with the big house in the suburbs, two late-model cars, and the fur coat. It had nothing to do with our love of money. It was an economic necessity. After all we were entitled!

> *Meaning doesn't lie in things. Meaning lies in us. When we attach value to things that aren't love — the money, the car, the house, the prestige — we are loving things that can't love us back. We are searching for meaning in the meaningless. Money, of itself, means nothing.*
>
> *Marianne Williamson, Contemporary Spiritual Leader of the Church Today, Co-founder of the Global Renaissance Alliance, and Author, from* A Return To Love

Recession Fallout

Crash, boom, bang! The industrial-era economy begins to crumble. Black Monday hit on October 19, 1987 — the first stock market crash since 1929. The combined forces of rising costs, increased competition, changing demographics, and advancing technology brought the giants of industry to their knees. No sector was spared — steel, oil, telecommunications, banking, consumer products, or health care. Demand for consumer goods was declining in the United States. Markets were becoming saturated. Most households had two or three televisions, a microwave oven, and a stove.

The population was aging, and there was declining demand for staples. The personal computer market was just beginning in the mid-'80s, and Americans did not yet know that every household was going to need one. The Japanese had embraced total quality management a full decade before it was on the radar screens of American companies. And while it was hard for us smug Americans to believe about our own selves, we sold out and began to purchase Japanese consumer electronics and cars. After all, the quality was far superior to our own products.

Companies could no longer sustain the large bureaucracies that they had built. Something drastic had to be done to remain competitive. Thus, the downsizing era emerged. The easiest and most tangible way to cut costs was to reduce labor — the largest and most direct expense. It was and still is a bitter pill to swallow.

Between 1993 and 1996, downsizing impacted millions of workers. We had hoped that downsizing was a one-time phenomenon. Baby boomers thought they could breathe a sigh of relief as the economy seemingly rebounded.

Even so, competition continued to be formidable and even the most successful companies found themselves needing to adjust workforce levels again at the beginning of the 21st century. According to the Bureau of Labor Statistics, between December 2000 and April 2001, one million workers were furloughed, and some of the biggest names in business topped the list of companies laying off workers.[18]

The cuts hit the automobile, telecommunications, and retail sectors the hardest, as shown in Figure 2.

Figure 2
Downsizings Between December 2000 and April 2001

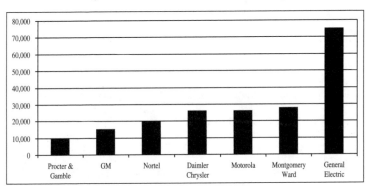

Source: CBS/MarketWatch.com (April 2001)[19]

Literally, millions of baby boomers have been displaced over the past 20 years as a result of the transformation of the economy. The cuts from the ranks of corporate America have not discriminated based on how much debt you have, the size of your savings account, or your retirement plans. And there is no end in sight. An already sagging economy, stunned by the September 11, 2001 terrorist attacks on the U.S., is struggling to get back on its feet in 2002. The fallout is more layoffs, especially in the airline, retail, and even technology industries.

While some of us are able to ride the waves of the economic roller coaster, many have had to accept lower-paying positions or have had to be retrained for other work. The good news is that being forced to rethink their careers has led many baby boomers to their passion work (see Chapter 8)—something that might not have happened as long as the good times kept rolling.

Take, for example, a massage therapist I met in St. Thomas, U.S. Virgin Islands. He had worked for Bethlehem Steel in Harrisburg, Pennsylvania, as a mechanic for 23 years. He was downsized and forced to retool. He became a certified personal trainer and masseur. He loves his work and relocated to the Caribbean, where he and his wife run a business.

> **It is important to me that money not be important to me.**
>
> *Les Brown, Contemporary Motivational Speaker and Author*

Compounding the issue of downsizing is the state of Social Security. Baby boomers were led to believe that they had an added security blanket to supplement whatever retirement plans their companies offered. "Think again," we now know. With the idea of government-sponsored retirement help fading, the baby boomers' predicament is even more precarious. By 2040, it is predicted that one in five Americans will be over 65 and eligible to receive their Social Security benefits.[20] The ratio of workers paying into the Social Security system to those eligible to receive benefits will be 2:1.[21] To put that figure in perspective, in 1940, five years after the Social Security system was created, that ratio was 159:1.[22]

As a result of the demise of job stability and secure retirement benefits and little savings, baby boomers expect to have to work longer than they might have originally planned.

Readjusting Our Attitudes

With our strong ideology that money and success are synonymous, baby boomers are in great emotional pain today as they wrestle with the new rules that eliminate entitlement and job security. Because of our strong activist roots, we believed that we could change our circumstances with protest and persistence. After all, we were the ones who changed an entire social order in the '60s. But our activist skills are a little rusty and our resolve a bit stale. We got a little too smug, comfortable, and complacent; we were caught off guard.

But this jolt allows us to rethink who we have become and what we value as a society. We don't even have to think long or hard to come to the conclusion that our economic prosperity did not really bring us the joy and personal fulfillment we sought. Why are we so disgruntled in our jobs? With our bosses? Why are we never content with our salaries? Why is it that we always feel we need more?

At The Winters Group, when we ask people in surveys how satisfied they are with their pay, invariably, it is one of the lower scores. Why is it that the bigger house or the more expensive car doesn't quite give us the feeling of euphoria that we are looking for? Have you noticed that with each material acquisition that we can make because we work longer and harder, we just don't feel quite as satisfied as we thought we would? So what do we do? The vicious cycle continues. We just keep striving to advance a little more because we know for sure that if we just had a little more money, we would be able to afford a little better this or that, which will lead to our complete jubilation this time.

> *He who is of the opinion that money will do every-thing, may well be suspected of doing everything for money.*
>
> *Benjamin Franklin, 18th-Century American Scientist, Inventor and Statesman*

It is a myth. It won't happen. More "stuff" will not lead to happiness and contentment. As baby boomers, we bought the myth "hook, line, and sinker" and now it is time to wake up. Our attitude that money equals success must change if we are to find that true "pot of gold." The pot of gold already exists inside of you. Sometimes it is buried so deeply with so much stuff piled on top of it that it will take a real concerted effort to find it. But when you do, you won't need to worry about money. Your inner prosperity will naturally lead to outer prosperity. When you find your own pot of gold, it will lead you to your passion work — that which you love to do. You will do it so well that compensation will be generously offered.

> *When I chased money, I never had enough. When I got my life on purpose and focused on giving of myself and everything that arrived in my life, then I was prosperous.*
>
> Wayne Dyer, *Contemporary American Spiritualist, Author, and Motivational Speaker*

I am suggesting that you completely redefine success for yourself and divorce it from any association with money.

Living a successful life is closer to what I described at the beginning of the chapter. I am not suggesting that you become a teacher, preacher, or funeral director, unless you are called to do so. But the point is that personal success is more about character, integrity, and knowing your unique purpose than it is about making more money.

Don't get me wrong. Money is a necessity and it is very nice to have more rather than less of it. What I am suggesting, however, is that we rethink what it means to us—to reposition the place money holds in our consciousness. Ask yourself, "Are you making the money or is the money making you?"

Over the past 15 years, several of my women friends have wanted to jump off the corporate ladder but could not see their way clear from a financial perspective. They have fallen into the "make-it and spend-it" trap. A few took the risk anyway, and in each case, they were surprised at how little their economic status really changed. They found other ways—less stressful and time-consuming—to earn an income using their gifts. And they discovered that with more time to attend to personal needs that they used to hire out, they could actually maintain their socioeconomic status.

The repositioning of the role of money in your life definitely does not mean that you have to lower your socioeconomic standards. It simply means that you control your life rather than money controlling you.

It is not too late for baby boomers. Many of us will be working another 20 years. We have the opportunity to reinvent ourselves, what we value, and the livelihood we choose.

Most of us were advised to get a "good job," which really meant one that paid the most money. I encourage you to find your "best livelihood"—one that brings the most personal prosperity.

If GenXers are more adept at handling the rapid pace of change, Generation Y (generally defined as individuals born from 1978 to 1986) may be even more conscious of the importance of finding their passion work. My GenY son and niece are examples. My son is a cum laude graduate of Harvard University with a degree in economics. My niece graduated with honors from Duke University with a degree in electrical engineering. Both, coincidentally, are in graduate school at Duke pursuing degrees in religion. My son came to me one day during his senior year at Harvard and said, "Mom, I don't want to go into business. I have had summer internships, but I just don't like that environment. I want to study religion. I know you are probably disappointed in me, and I probably won't ever make a lot of money..." At that moment, I was more proud of him than I had ever been. I hugged him tightly and said, "Follow your passion, my son." He is currently pursuing a doctorate in comparative religious studies.

My niece had summer internships in business as well and had several lucrative offers when she graduated. She, too, did not find personal fulfillment from her engineering experiences. It took a great deal of courage and self-awareness to turn completely from what our current societal values would have considered a great opportunity to follow her calling.

I sometimes get an interesting reaction to my son and niece's educational pursuits. Some of my baby boomer compatriots question why these two obviously bright young people have selected careers where their earning potential in terms of dollars is limited relative to a business career. One of the most telling comments was, "Don't worry. I am sure that they will get back on track." What track? By whose measure of success?

Reframing your view of success will take not only a great deal of soul-searching, but will also mean changing years of spending behaviors. Resolve to get out of debt completely, not to spend more than you need to, and save aggressively.

> *Don't let your wants exceed your needs.*
>
> *Joseph R. Winters, Sr., the Author's Late Husband*

This is not a book about financial planning, but there are great resources on the market to help you with that. Nobody is in so much debt or is so far out of control that the trend can't be reversed. The first and most important reversal, though, is your attitude about money and success. Be aware of your real attitude about money and the place it holds in the decisions you make for your life. Only when you know what your attitude is (Be honest!) can you decide if you want to change it. If you no longer worship money and if you discontinue your love affair with it, the new behaviors will be easier.

> *Try not to be a person of success but rather a person of value.*
>
> *Albert Einstein, 20th-Century German Scientist and Mathematician*

Affirmation: I will not worship money. I will not equate money with success. I will get my financial house in order and pursue my best livelihood not based on earning potential but on my passion and calling. Prosperity is inevitable when I choose from within.

Summary of Key Points:

- Value systems shifted abruptly in the '70s, equating success almost solely with financial status.

- Boomers were at the center of the social revolution in the late '60s and early '70s.

- Affirmative action opened professional doors, previously not available, to women and people of color, in the '70s.

- Some boomers sold out their ideals for greed.

- "Make it, spend it," is a mentality that has characterized our generation.

- The New Economy is forcing all of us to rethink how we view money, career, and self.

- It is not too late to adjust your attitude about what defines success and what defines you.

Ask Yourself:

1. Who were the professionals my family and I most admired when I was growing up?

2. How did I decide on a career path? What really motivated me?

3. How did the '60s and '70s impact my choices and shape my values?

4. Did I spend more liberally than my parents? Do I save well? Am I in debt today?

5. Am I truly satisfied with my current job? Am I fulfilled?

6. Has another career always been the "calling" I haven't dared to pursue?

7. Am I willing to rethink how I spend and save in order to pursue other career options?

8. Do I have the courage to step out on faith to create the life and livelihood that I want?

Chapter 3

Walk With Yourself

Self-knowledge comes too late and by the time I've known myself I am no longer what I was.

Mabel Segun, Contemporary Author, from
Reflections: Nigerian Prose and Verse

Now that you have a context for how baby boomers' values and attitudes have shaped the course of history, the balance of the book will take you through a journey of self-reflection and introspection. Who am I? Have I found my authentic self? What are some of the manifestations in the workplace that impact me? How do I respond to change? What do I do to discover and unleash my gifts? What do I have to learn, unlearn, and relearn to find fulfillment in the rest of my working years?

Boomers' focus on acquiring material wealth contributed to losing touch with the true essence of our beings. But our roots in activism and social change should prepare us well for the transformation that I advocate. Hopefully, we have some recollection of our values and beliefs back in the '60s and '70s even though the memory of those things, I am finding, is in an inverse relationship with age.

The first step in embracing change is embracing yourself totally and completely. In order to change your mindset, you have to know your mindset. Writers, philosophers, religious leaders, and behavioral scientists have advocated for centuries that knowing self is the secret to all other success. Why is it then, that in 2002, the message is still so painfully needed? Why don't we, as a rule, really work on knowing ourselves? Why do we need coaches, counselors, and therapists to crack the code to understanding self? There are myriad reasons why people tend to shy away from looking deep in the mirror.

> *There has never been another you. With no effort on your part you were born to be something very special and set apart. What you are going to do in appreciation for that gift is a decision only you can make.*
>
> Dan Zadra, Contemporary Inspirational Author, Publisher, and Strategic Communications Consultant

For me, the main obstacle was allowing myself to be unduly influenced by others. I had a tendency to compare myself to others—to copy their approach in an attempt to conform to some arbitrary mainstream standard. What I thought became secondary to what others thought about me or for me. I spent so much time trying to be what I thought I needed to be in order to succeed (Yeah, the money thing!), that I lost my sense of self. I did not think about what I really wanted, what gave me the most joy, and how I could best contribute to the world during my brief stay here. I had no sense of personal mission.

When I started my career in corporate America in the mid-'70s, I was hired in the first wave of the affirmative action movement. There was strong pressure to conform. As a matter of fact, the company sent me to a program called The Association for the Integration of Management (AIM). As I reflect on the content of the workshop, it was designed to train us how to act and behave to be accepted by the culture, which was, of course, primarily white male. We were advised to be conservative in dress and hairstyle, not to display too many family pictures in our offices, and not to congregate at the water cooler as it might be threatening. I wore a short natural hairstyle at the time, and I remember vividly when one of my managers asked me if my hair would grow. When I said "Of course," he suggested that I let it! There was no room for diversity of expression, style, thinking, or approach in the early days of my corporate experience.

I sometimes felt schizophrenic—split with one personality for work and another for the rest of my life. I would drive to work each day and practice how I needed to act that day. One manager rated my performance as "too aggressive;" the next manager advised that I needed to be more "assertive." I was totally confused and not contributing my very best because I was too busy expending energy on adjusting myself to fit "the standard." I knew I needed to conform in order to "succeed," but had very little understanding of exactly what that meant.

I did not focus on developing my own talents and gifts because I felt that I would only be rewarded for emulating somebody else. I lost 11 years of opportunity to grow in self-knowledge in corporate America because I did not have the courage or self-esteem to show up as "me." I did not really know who "me" was, and I was not trying to find her. I had no sense that I had a divine purpose and unique gifts, or that I could pursue my passion.

The Fallacy of the Four C's

The four C's that can keep us from self-understanding are: copying, competing, comparing, and conforming. Each of us, to some extent, falls prey to the four C's.

We copy by looking at the steps someone took to achieve career success and embracing his or her model. Just because it worked for someone else does not mean the same steps will work for you. It is okay to use the path of another as input, but to assume that you can simply follow a magic "recipe" and the outcome will be the same is not wise. The "inputs" are different for each of us. Inputs such as personality, innate gifts, and experience are unique. When we blindly copy another's path, we are often disappointed that the outcome is not the same for us. Message: Develop and follow your own path.

In post-modern America, competition—the second C— is firmly rooted in our value system. The free enterprise system and open markets are concepts that we strongly embrace. Competition in the business world for market share is fierce today. That same competitive spirit is fostered in individuals. You have to be better than, smarter than, more articulate than, more educated than your co-worker. In our personal lives, we strive to have bigger houses, better cars, and memberships to more exclusive clubs than our neighbors. Our motivation to compete is often misguided if it is simply to win for winning's sake, so I can declare "I am better than you."

From early childhood, we are taught that the world is about winning and losing. In sports, in school, in dance class, in music lessons, in any endeavor in which we engage our children, there is competition. Striving for excellence is certainly admirable, but sometimes our motivations are not. Motivations rooted in jealousy and mean-spiritedness—where we would do harm to another for our gain—fosters dishonest, unethical and even illegal behavior. We've seen numerous examples of the downfall of business, political, and religious leaders, who allowed their competitive yearnings to get out of hand in their quest to have more, more, and more (see Chapter 2).

Healthy competition spurs us to achieve to our potential, but is only possible when you know yourself and have a high self-concept—when you are principled and live the values you espouse. Highly principled people set their goals based on their own personal vision and mission, not those of others. Highly self-actualized people compete with themselves more often than with others. They seek win/win scenarios, rather than win/lose. They engage in behaviors that benefit not only themselves, but others as well.

73

The third C that impedes our progress to self-understanding is "comparing." We judge our situation relative to others. We compare, assess, and decide to compete for what we perceive to be the "one-up" position, if we don't already have it. I spent most of my adult life comparing my circumstances to others. It actually started in college. Growing up in a homogeneous working class environment, I did not understand the "class" system until I left home for college. I did not know that I was relatively poor (from an economic perspective) compared to my classmates from suburban Long Island. Where we get hung up in comparing is putting value judgments—better/worse or good/bad—on our circumstances. "I'm not as good as...as smart as...as wealthy as..." Focusing on what others have keeps us from developing our own gifts. It is true that we do not possess the attributes, characteristics, and circumstances of others. Each of us is differently gifted.

Comparing is useful if we are assessing gifts and talents in an attempt to optimize team performance, for example. Comparing is not useful when it results in the devaluing of one person's gifts in favor of another's. We can see this happening in families fairly often, "Why can't you be more like your brother?" In organizations, the favorite phrase is: "We need more employees just like Mary."

Resist comparing yourself to others. It will only increase your frustration and impede your journey to understanding self. Examine yourself in absolute rather than relative terms. "What are my special talents?" Not, "What am I better at than Mary?"

The last C is "conforming." We can't help ourselves. We are forced in our society to "try to fit in," "don't rock the boat," "don't be too different," "find out how the game is played and play it." I have already described the pressure I faced to conform in corporate America. Where would we be today if Susan B. Anthony had conformed? If Martin Luther King, Jr., or Nelson Mandela had conformed? If Columbus, Magellan, or any of the early explorers had conformed? Obviously, there are certain boundaries of decorum. I am not advocating what is considered deviant behavior. But preoccupation with trying to fit into an arbitrary standard of acceptable behavior, thought, and attitudes contributes to our denial of self.

> *What another would have done as well as you, do not do it. What another would have said as well as you, do not say it; written as well, do not write it. Be faithful to that which exists nowhere but in yourself... and there make yourself indispensable.*
>
> *André Gide, 20th-Century French Writer*

The first step in walking with yourself is to be clear about what you stand for—your values and principles—those things for which you will not compromise.

Examine Turning Points to Uncover Values

So how does one achieve deeper self-knowledge? Going deeper means understanding how the sum of your life's experiences has shaped your values, your principles, and your essence. It is exploring how your upbringing, early environment, education, work, and faith experiences impact who you are. For example, how has being of the baby boom generation influenced who you are? How did being an affirmative action hire impact who I am today? We don't often go back into our early childhood and past life experiences to reflect on how our values have been shaped. It is an awe-inspiring exercise.

I worked with life coach, Juanell Teague of People Plus Inc., in Dallas, Texas, about five years ago, and she introduced me to the concept of "turning points." These are significant events in your life that have such a dramatic impact on you that they shape your values and your very being. My life coach had me think of as many turning points as possible from early childhood to identify what core value each turning point shaped. Understanding your turning points is a significant way to better understand self. We cannot reach our full potential without understanding self. We cannot embrace change well without deep self-understanding. We will probably never fully understand all of the complexities of what makes each of us unique. Ongoing examination of those significant events that have shaped our values will move us closer to self-understanding and the ability to reach new heights.

We can all remember significant events in our lives that we would call turning points — those life-altering revelations that gave us new understanding, provided the impetus for change, allowed us to release anger, to forgive, and to love again. Turning points may have changed our careers or our relationships; they may have helped us understand ourselves better as well as our true gifts to the world. And turning points may have brought us from the depths of despair to new visions of hope.

Many of us do not think about these turning points in the aggregate and how each had a role in shaping our core values. What are core values, you might ask? For me, core values are those unspoken beliefs that drive behavior. They are what you care about most deeply in your subconscious. They are not seen or spoken, but they are the essence of your being. They may be moral or ethical in nature. Values may be about the spiritual, the emotional, and/or the intellectual. Values shape our personalities and make us uniquely "us." Values emerge from our experiences and turning points.

I had never thought about a kindergarten experience as a turning point that shaped one of my core values before my session with the life coach. I remember this early experience as if it happened yesterday. I grew up in Niagara Falls, New York, and lived in a fairly homogeneous working class, white neighborhood. The two-block Ely Avenue, where we lived, was almost entirely black, but all of the streets around it were white, primarily Italian. The neighborhood has changed over the years, and black families now primarily inhabit several contiguous streets. But back in 1956 when I entered kindergarten at 39th Street School, there was only one other black student in the class, my friend Charlene. We walked to school together every day. We played together. Our mothers were best friends and so were we.

On one ordinary day, Charlene and I were in the coatroom when a co-kindergartner, named Billy, bounded in and said, "Look at the niggers, na, na, na, na, na." Charlene and I looked at each other in astonishment. We had not heard that word before, but we knew it must have been bad because of the tone of Billy's voice. We started to cry. Our teacher heard our plea, and came running into the coatroom with her hand on her hips: "What in the world is wrong with you girls? Why are you crying?" By this time, Billy had vacated the scene of the crime. We told our teacher what happened and she immediately called Billy in, pointed her finger at him and said, "Your red hair is ugly and your freckles are too!" With that, Billy started to cry. Now all three of us were crying. I am not sure that our teacher's approach would pass a Dr. Spock test today, but Charlene and I felt that somehow justice had been served.

That was the first time that I really understood that I was different, and that my difference made a difference. That was a turning point!

My first real recollection of my childhood starts with that kindergarten experience. At five years old, I had a rude awakening from my naiveté and youthful innocence. The color of your skin makes you different, and some people don't like you because of it.

Imagine a five-year-old child trying to process what this meant—trying as hard as I might to understand why brown was not as good as white—trying as hard as I might to understand why Billy would not like us, simply because we looked different than him. After all, he looked different, too. His red hair and freckles set him apart. But somehow that difference was okay. Charlene's and mine were not. Imagine a five-year-old child trying to understand such complexities. Imagine the impact on a five-year-old child's self-concept.

My mother was honest with me when I told her the Billy story. She told me that some people were prejudiced and did not like "colored" people. (In 1956 blacks and African Americans were still called "colored.") Even though "prejudiced" was a big word for a kindergartner, I understood the definition because I had just had a real-life experience with it.

This kindergarten turning point made me cautious, suspicious, and unsure of myself. From that point, I was labeled as shy by family and friends because I no longer felt free to express myself and to explore my little world for fear that someone would question my right to do so.

The life coach asked me what core value this turning point helped to form, and I reflected it was respect for self and others. You see, I had to experience self-doubt in order to learn to love and respect myself. I learned the self-doubting behavior as a result of my encounter with Billy. In understanding the root cause of the doubt, I was better equipped to take the necessary steps to alleviate it. I still have self-doubts (not as many as I used to, though) when I go into new situations. I often need an encouraging, supportive word from family or friends to give me the courage to be "me" and do it my way and not the way I think somebody else might want it done.

My "Billy" experience also impacted my sense of fairness and justice. Knowing how it feels to be hated because of what you look like has impassioned me to be an activist — to challenge boldly the traditions, beliefs, and conventions that keep some people from being all that they are capable of being.

A very significant adult turning point was starting my own business.

> *We have flown the air like birds and swum the sea like fishes, but have yet to learn the simple act of walking the earth like brothers.*
>
> *Martin Luther King, Jr.*

I left corporate America on March 16, 1984, with the annual bonus check that all employees received from the company for which I worked. I did not know if I would ever earn an income again; however, I did know that on the day I walked out the door, I felt like a bird whose cage had been opened after many years of captivity. I was free to fly. I was free to be me. I was free from corporate politics and etiquette — free to explore my interests — free to challenge myself — free to pursue my passion.

> *It is not because things are difficult that we do not dare, it is because we do not dare that things are difficult.*
>
> *Seneca, Roman Philosopher (3 B.C. – 65 A.D.)*

I was a little ahead of the curve as a woman starting her own business. It was not until the late '80s that many more women jumped off the corporate ladder in favor of a more flexible, fulfilling career. I had no idea what I was doing or what I was going to do beyond the small contract I had from my former employer.

I did not have a business plan (not a very smart move). I was going to be a consultant in a variety of areas. I felt that I had a variety of talents that I could offer. On that first day, I sat at my newly purchased Macintosh® computer in my basement office and wrote letters to practically everyone I ever knew. I was tempted to include my kindergarten teacher, but I thought that might be going a little too far.

The work began to pour in. I received calls from several companies asking about my capabilities. Can you write speeches? Do you do telephone surveys? What about your experience in conducting focus groups? Strategic planning? Training? I said "yes" to all of it. Of course I could do it all. I could do anything I set my mind to and do it well, couldn't I?

I was so overwhelmed with projects that I got up some mornings at 3 a.m. to begin working. My neighbor asked one day what I was doing at the kitchen table in a pink robe so early in the morning. (I wondered what she was doing up so early!) I sent my family on vacation by themselves. I had too much work to do.

About six months into the business, I decided that I could not do it all well by myself. I needed an assistant. With much trepidation, I hired a part-time assistant. I was so afraid of failing. Could I afford to pay someone on an ongoing basis?

About 10 months into the business, it became apparent that I needed even more people. I continued to tell everybody who asked, "Can you...?" the same answer: "Yes, I can!" I started to hire college students to help do research, collect data, and handle other duties that I had not anticipated. (Remember: I had no business plan.)

I moved into a tiny office on my first anniversary with two full-time employees. The business continued to grow. I was truly blessed. I had passed that magical one-year point. I continued to hire people. By the end of the second year, I had people working in the hallway of the office building. We finally moved into larger quarters.

At my peak, I had 20 employees and about 5,000 square feet of office space. I was out of control! (Remember: I had no business plan.) I put together an advisory board. One of the board's first questions was, "What does The Winters Group do?" I stuttered and said, "Lots of things." One seasoned businessperson offered: "That's your problem. You need to have a focus."

Since most of our business appeared to be in the market research area, I decided to position the business as a market research firm. I developed a business plan and tried to follow it. The tag line for The Winters Group became: "Helping businesses make better decisions with information."

I had developed no infrastructure for 20 people. There was low morale, confusion, and poor quality. The contracts stopped coming in, and I was spiraling towards disaster.

I was not going to give up, though. I had found my passion! I loved the independence of owning my own business. Despite the internal problems, I had gained respect in the community and was active in a number of civic, not-for-profit and philanthropic endeavors.

I downsized to 10 people, enhanced quality, and developed human resource policies and other internal controls. It helped immensely. We were back on track and the business was profitable again.

Then the recession of the early '90s hit. The first services that corporations cut were advertising, market research, and training. Here I was again in a downturn—bills to pay and no funds. I had no choice but to downsize again. In the course of this downsizing, I really began to think about my passion and what I really liked to do. Was I in the market research business because I loved it or because somebody said, "You need a focus"? Did I want to manage people? Did I want to be consumed by my business 24/7?

I did some significant soul-searching in 1994, reviewing

what I had accomplished over the 10 years that I had been in business. I had shown the naysayers—the ones who doubted my capabilities. I had earned the respect of the business world and had received many awards and honors to prove it. I was seeking more challenge than the corporate world afforded me, and, oh, did I get it. Running a business is the ultimate challenge.

But what about me personally? Had I done anything that I was proud of to develop myself spiritually? What about my relationships with friends and family?

I realized that I had spent the last decade building a business and trying to prove something to the doubters. I was not achieving because of my own personal passion for the work. I was not driving myself 70 to 80 hours a week because I was energized and excited by the work. I was driven by proving, to anybody who would dare question me with the slightest bit of skepticism, that I could do it. My motivation was to show all of those people who had ever said "you can't" or "you shouldn't" that they were wrong.

> *For what does it profit a man if he gains the world but loses his soul.*
>
> The Bible, King James Version, Mark 8:36

But what did I stand for? Who had I become? What did I want? Who was I? People admired me for my business acumen but what about me as a person? Did anybody really know me? Did I allow anyone to really know me? Did I really know any of my friends and colleagues—what was important to them—what they stood for? I was totally consumed by measuring up to the standards that had been set by the white male business world. Whatever any business colleague said was right, good, and true, I accepted without question. I wanted to be accepted. Why? Just to be able to say that I was—not necessarily because I enjoyed the experience.

If you listen though, God sends you messages. Someone I did not know came up to me after a speech I delivered and said, "I have been following you since you left corporate America. You are a true inspiration to many of us. You have helped me immensely in my career. I have read the articles about you, and you have motivated me to stay focused on my dreams. I have finished college and am now in a professional career—something I never thought I could do. Thank you."

I was flabbergasted. I had no idea that I could have such an impact on someone that I did not know. I was certainly not consciously trying to be a role model. I was self-absorbed with my obsession to show the white power structure that I had what it took. After that encounter, I decided to accept more of the speaking engagements that did not pay. If it was for a group of young people or others who were asking me to share my experiences and to help them unleash their potential, I would do it.

I am always "on a high" after speaking to a group of individuals and feeling their energy and anticipation. It is always enlightening for me as well. I learn so much from my audiences. They share their insights and wisdom, and I invariably leave with new understanding. When audience members come up to me after a presentation and vow to follow their deferred dreams or they embellish one of my points so that I am enriched with new perceptions, it makes it all worthwhile. Sharing and connecting with others in the spirit moves each of us to a higher purpose.

I have been richly blessed and I now know that, "to whom much is given, much is required." Even though my early motivations for success may have been misguided (my obsession to prove something to somebody else and make a lot of money), God allowed much good to come from it. I unwittingly helped others and now realize that when I give of myself, I get back much more than I gave.

> *Do not spill thy soul running hither and yon, grieving over the mistakes and the vices of others; the one person whom it is most necessary to reform is yourself.*
>
> *Ralph Waldo Emerson, 19th-Century American Essayist, Poet, and Philosopher*

I have refocused my business. I have one full-time administrative assistant and another part-timer to keep the fixed costs down and allow me the flexibility to explore and expand my potential. But I am able to conduct the same

91

level of business by working with about 10 strategic part-ners—other consultants. We work together as a networked, virtual corporation to deliver high-quality services to clients. My mission now reads: "Inspiring organizational ingenuity from the workplace to the marketplace." My key assumption is that everybody and every organization has a spark of genius and excellence. It is a matter of believing it, finding it, developing it, and nurturing it.

Whether I am addressing a room full of cynical corporate employees, a group of recent college graduates, a group of aspiring entrepreneurs, or helping a group of senior managers develop a strategic plan, my message is the same: "You can do abundantly more that you think you can today if you get in touch with your spirit, know who you are, step out on faith, and never compromise."

A large part of my consulting business is conducting diversity training and strategy development. I resisted moving into this arena. A typical field for a black woman: diversity consulting! I did not want to be labeled. I remembered my early corporate days as an affirmative action officer. I trained employees in the legal aspects of affirmative action and represented the company in discrimination suits. I felt a sense of conflict as an African American defending the company.

The thought of trying to convince people that discrimination and racism still exist in our society was not very appealing. Yet, something kept pulling me to this work. At first, it was about business but I began to realize that I was making some small difference. I understood that valuing diversity concepts had nothing to do with affirmative action. Valuing diversity was about respecting every individual for his or her uniqueness. In the workplace, the goal has become to create an environment where every individual can reach his or her full potential.

I began to understand that diversity concepts know no gender or racial boundaries. Diversity truly is about seeing everyone's uniqueness as a beautiful gift to be nurtured and developed, not changed to conform to some arbitrary standard. I began to understand that if we could find that kernel of excellence, individual productivity would surely be enhanced.

As participants in those sessions, even white men, started to approach me and declare that it had been years since anybody acknowledged and encouraged their uniqueness — that it had been a long time, and for some, no one had ever said, "You have something special to offer."

> *I refuse to accept the idea that the "isness" of man's present nature makes him morally incapable of reaching up for the "oughtness" that forever confronts him.*
>
> *Martin Luther King, Jr.*

I realized that if I could help even one person recognize that the power to achieve resides within, that our diversity makes us stronger, that there is a place just for you next to your "brother/sister," co-worker, and neighbor who has his or her own special talent to offer that is different from yours, then I was truly making my unique contribution.

On the dawn of The Winters Group's 10th anniversary, I awoke at 5 a.m., sat down at the computer, and within 45 minutes had written the following. It sums up my philosophy on diversity and how humankind can work together while valuing, celebrating, and tapping our uniqueness.

Our spirits are inextricably entwined.

No matter where we have been on our individual journeys on this earth or where we are going, we are One.

The beauty of our humanness comes from the breadth of our diversity . . .
The depths of our individuality and the wholeness and creative synergy that comes from the bringing together of each individual's special God-sent gifts.

The miracle rainbow that symbolizes our differences also shows us that when we are arced together in unison we make a beautiful and lasting impression.

When we lift our voices in harmony the resulting sound of each unique pitch creates a melodious effect that no one voice is capable of.

We must find the loving spirit that dwells deep inside of each of us . . . That spirit which compels us to care . . . to serve . . . to share . . . Which brings forth agape, and provides the capacity for a change of heart.

*We must come to a greater understanding of our
connectedness. We do not exist outside of the universe.
We do not exist separate from other life forms,
from other peoples of the world.*

*We must see the wisdom in creating new linkages —
the power that emerges from combining our energy as we
strive to attain our universal vision.*

*A vision of respect for all humankind . . .
A vision drawn from our interconnectedness and
enlightened by the spirit, mind, and body.*

Starting and growing a business was a monumental challenge for me. I have had many turning points during the 18 years that I have been in business. I have learned much. And I know that there is much more to learn.

The values that this turning point nurtured were spirituality and faith, together with personal freedom and independence.

This turning point taught me that you can only truly be self-fulfilled and reach your full potential if you listen to your heart (spirit) and follow your true passions, not some-body else's.

> *I think somehow we learn who we really are and then live with that decision.*
>
> *Eleanor Roosevelt, Wife of Franklin D. Roosevelt,*
> *32nd President of the United States*

Examining Core Values

Reflecting on turning points can help to surface your core values—those lessons learned, sometimes the hard way, that become the foundation of our belief system. We don't often think about our personal values, although we live them every day.

Rushworth M. Kidder, president and founder of the Institute for Global Ethics and author of several books, including *Shared Values for a Troubled World: Conversations with Men and Women of Conscience,* interviewed 24 opinion makers in 16 countries in an effort to identify global core values— a "global code of ethics comprised of eight moral values."

The values to which people subscribe, irrespective of race, gender, religion, or culture include: truthfulness, love, freedom, fairness, unity, tolerance, responsibility, and respect for life.[1]

While most of us would not argue with the merit of all of these values, some may be more important to you than others. In an exercise created by life coach Juanell Teague, you rank your core values as outlined in the sample survey in Figure 3. In exploring what is most important to us, we can begin to ask ourselves whether our behavior is consistent with what we say our core values are. We can also examine the extent to which our values are consistent with the values of the organization for which we work.

Figure 3
Core Values Exercise

In column 1, put an "X" next to your top 10 core values. In the second column, prioritize the 10 you selected, where 1 equals the most important, 2 the second most important, 3 the third most important and so on until you get to 10.

Column 1 Column 2

____	____	1.	Accumulation of wealth
____	____	2.	Financial security
____	____	3.	Respect
____	____	4.	Recognition — to be well-known to other people
____	____	5.	Personal freedom and independence
____	____	6.	Family structure and cohesiveness
____	____	7.	Spirituality and faith
____	____	8.	Organized and clean structure of environment
____	____	9.	Organized structure of personal routine and schedule
____	____	10.	Punctuality for self
____	____	11.	Efficient use of time
____	____	12.	Personal solitude
____	____	13.	Power
____	____	14.	Creativity
____	____	15.	Continuous learning
____	____	16.	To be appreciated
____	____	17.	Good health
____	____	18.	Challenge
____	____	19.	To experience excitement and adventure
____	____	20.	To compete
____	____	21.	To be productive
____	____	22.	Inner peace
____	____	23.	Love and affection
____	____	24.	Service to others
____	____	25.	To interact with others
____	____	26.	To gain wisdom and insight
____	____	27.	To enjoy cultural activities
____	____	28.	To have intimate (truly honest and close) relationships with others

Adapted with permission from People Plus, Inc.©

What are your top 10 values?

The prioritization of your values may change over time. I completed this exercise in 1995, and at that time my top values were: (1) productivity; (2) service to others; (3) interaction with others; (4) wisdom and insight; (5) spirituality and faith; (6) family structure and cohesiveness, along with intimate relationships with others. If I were to complete the exercise today, my top values would be: (1) spirituality and faith; (2) personal freedom and independence; (3) family structure; (4) inner peace; (5) intimate relationships, and (6) wisdom and insight.

As you journey through life, what you value changes, based on those turning point experiences. I think spirituality and faith are "number one" for me at this stage in my life as a result of witnessing so many miracles in the last five years that were manifested even in the wake of tremendous pain and sadness.

Sometimes our personal values are incongruous with those of our employer. When our personal values and convictions are deeply rooted, it is easy for us to identify the areas of conflict. When they are not, it can lead to a greater level of confusion and frustration in the workplace. We are also more apt to conform "blindly" when we are not clear about our values. When you have a firm sense of self and are clear on your principles, it is not difficult to make personal choices.

> *Say not, I have found the truth, but rather, I have found a truth. Say not I have found the path of the soul. Say rather, I have met the soul walking upon my path. For the soul walks upon all paths. The soul walks not upon a line, neither does it grow like a reed. The soul unfolds itself, like a lotus of countless petals.*
>
> *Kahlil Gibran, 20th-Century Lebanese Poet, Philosopher and Artist, from The Prophet*

Seek Self-Differentiation

Knowing your core values is a prerequisite to understanding yourself and how you are different from other people in your life.

Many of us see ourselves in relationship to others, as I did when I was working in corporate America. As pointed out earlier in this chapter, we have a tendency to compare, copy, compete, and conform.

If we put our energy into focusing on others, we miss out on knowing who we are. Our energy should be spent on self-discovery. You would be amazed at all of the hidden nuggets of brilliance you would find not only for yourself, but to share with others in your life.

> *We forfeit three-fourths of ourselves to be like other people.*
>
> *Arthur Schopenhauer, 19th-Century German Philosopher*

Murray Bowen, a psychotherapist who developed what is now known as Bowen Systems Theory, coined the term "self-differentiation" to help us reflect on self.[2] The concept of self-differentiation is just one aspect of a more holistic theory about how all organisms respond in an emotional system. My friend and colleague, Frank Staropoli, president of Staropoli Consulting, is an expert in Bowen Systems Theory and has supported the lay understanding of how to use these concepts to help individuals and organizations facing dramatic change.

Basically, self-differentiation is the ability to shape a concept of self as distinct from others. It is the ability to function as an individual while still being able to relate to others. Highly self-differentiated people focus on their own functioning in stressful situations rather than on what others are doing or not doing. They experience life more as a series of choices, rather than as events over which they have no control. Self-respect increases in direct proportion to the amount of self that is claimed.

Self-differentiation is possible for those who have a great deal of self-knowledge. A highly self-differentiated person usually responds well to change. In an organizational or family setting, the less self-differentiation there is, the more dysfunction there is likely to be. For example, in a family of low individual self-differentiation, an offspring may connect to an alcoholic father and believe that to be his or her fate—something over which there is no control. Or, he or she may blame himself or herself in some way for the father's problem. In organizations where there are low levels of self-differentiation, subordinates may try to "be just like the boss" because they believe such behavior will be rewarded. "I want to find out what the boss wants and what kinds of personalities he likes so I can try to be like that." Chances are these individuals will not offer their best work because they give up self to try to be something they are not. When things don't work out, the boss is blamed for "making them" be a certain way.

Self-differentiation does not mean "weird" or strange. It is simply the ability for one to stay firm in his or her convictions and values, to be able to empathize with others, respect others' views, but not move from your own. It is about knowing your own values and beliefs and having a strong sense of personal purpose.

The personal decision-making process to determine if you can continue in an environment that is inconsistent with your belief system is easier for highly self-differentiated, self-knowledgeable people than for those who have yielded to the temptation of total conformity and of giving up self.

What are your core values? Which ones are not negotiable? A dear friend of mine coined a phrase as a New Year's resolution a few years ago: "No pretenses, no compromises." For what things do you unequivocally say, "No pretenses, no compromises"?

Seek Spirit

> **Soul is the indefinable essence of a person's spirit and being.**
>
> David Whyte, *Contemporary Poet, from* The Heart Aroused

If we dig deeper to know ourselves — into our souls — we can release the encumbrances that hold us hostage to mediocrity.

We are embarking on a new world, which is characterized by monumental change in the way we work, play, and interact with each other. Technological advances are occurring at lightning speed and afford us capabilities that we never thought imaginable. While this technological revolution is unfolding, it appears to result in the death of spirit for too many people.

The 21st century will require us to continue our technological advances. But there is little argument that we also need to build a caring, compassionate, and civil society that maximizes the unique gifts each individual has to offer, if only they are uncovered, unleashed, developed, and valued.

> *You are, in essence, spirit, housed in a physical envelope, brought to life by the breath of God to fulfill a divine mission.*
>
> Iyanla Vanzant, *Contemporary American Spiritualist and Author*

We have done an admirable job in the last century focusing on the development of the mind (formal education, continuous learning) and body (healthy eating, exercise), but have neglected the spirit. Discussions of spirit are scary for some because they conjure up notions of religion or our dark side and aspects of our being that we will never fully understand. To be complete and reach our highest level of existence, however, all three aspects of our humanness must be acknowledged, explored, and nurtured.

Getting in touch with yourself—elevating your self-knowledge—means working on not only the mind and the body but the spirit, that unknown place that drives our thinking, our behavior, and our very being.

> *Be melting snow. Wash yourself of yourself.*
>
> *Rumi, 13th-Century Muslim Poet*

I have personally witnessed the power of spirit. I have lost my way and experienced the wells of resources that are not on the surface and that are only available to those willing to risk the unknown, the dark places. It is not possible without a complete focus on self—not a narcissistic focus but a self-discovery, a self-caring focus. It is not possible unless you are willing to face the demons that we all suppress and try to ignore. It is in the soul that the true essence of self is housed. You cannot unleash the real, authentic, unique self without going to these depths. You have to be ready to deal with what you find. Once exposed, you cannot close it up and go back to business as usual. Once revealed, you must reckon with the essence of yourself. There may be healing of past hurts, conflicting values, and other issues that need professional help.

You have to take the first, sometimes difficult, step. If you are looking for the easy solution, the quick fix, don't go on this path. Remember: Anything that is worthwhile requires some pain and suffering.

Our unique gift to the universe might be buried in the soul, where we are afraid to go. Each one of us was given a special gift that many of us never find because it can only be discovered if we seek the spirit. It is a lifelong journey, my friends. We can only begin it by beginning. We have to desire greater depth of understanding of self, and then we have to begin the hard work—little by little, like peeling the layers of an onion until we get to the core.

The human spirit is so great a thing that no man can express it; could we rightly comprehend the mind of man nothing would be impossible to us upon this earth.

Paracelsus, 15th-Century German Physician and Chemist

Walking with yourself is a lifelong journey. Sometimes you are behind yourself. Sometimes you are ahead of yourself. And sometimes you don't know where you are. You are lost. Developing a keen sense of self will help you stay aligned and in step with yourself. Focusing on self is neither arrogant nor self-centered. You have an awesome responsibility in venturing to know self. It is not easy. It truly is our life's work. Knowing self enables us to unleash our best self as we experience and revel in life's limitless possibilities.

> *Knowing others is intelligence; knowing yourself is true wisdom. Mastering others is strength; mastering yourself is true power. If you realize you have enough, you are truly rich.*
>
> Tao Te Ching, Classic Book of Chinese Philosophy
> Written Between the 6th and 3rd Centuries B.C.

Affirmation: I will commit to knowing myself to the depths of my soul and knowing what makes me uniquely "me." I will seek to self-differentiate.

Summary of Key Points:

- Some of us baby boomers lost the essence of self with our obsession with material acquisitions.

- Self-knowledge is key today to coping effectively with the fast pace of change.

- It is human nature to copy, compare, conform, and compete with others rather than to discover our own unique gifts.

- Our core values are unspoken and under the surface but manifest in our behavior. They dictate how we are perceived by others.

- Self-differentiation allows us to function better in stressful situations.

- Examining key turning points in our lives leads to understanding our values and how we have become who we are.

- "Walking with self" is a lifelong journey.

Ask Yourself:

1. What steps have I taken to really know myself?

2. Am I afraid to go deep within to understand what makes me really "me"?

3. What have been the key turning points in my life that have shaped my values?

4. How self-differentiated am I?

5. When faced with change, do I tend to project blame to others or do I assess my own functioning in the situation?

6. Who am I? What do I stand for? For what am I not willing to compromise?

7. How do I express my uniqueness?

8. Do I always believe that I have choices?

Chapter 4
Step Out in Faith

Faith is the substance of things hoped and the evidence of things not seen.

The Bible, *King James Version, Hebrews 11:1*

Stepping out in faith is one of my core values, but faith without a plan is foolhardy. Faith, without knowing who you truly are and what you truly want to be and stand for, is naive.

How do you reveal your soul? Many of us find it through our expression of faith. Believers in a source of power that is omnipotent, omnipresent, and all encompassing let go and let spirit reign.

We can't see spirit but we know that it exists. We are aware of many accounts of miracles, things that we have evidence of but which cannot be explained by modern science. We see what we believe. No, I did not write it wrong. I know the popular saying goes, "We believe what we see." If we believe that we can start a business, we are able to see the vision. If we believe in miracles, we see them all around us.

It has been well documented over the past five years that people with a strong faith in a higher power heal faster and have better survival rates from serious illnesses. For example, a 1995 study of 232 heart surgery patients conducted by the Dartmouth Hitchcock Medical Center revealed that faith was a primary predictor of survival. The more a patient drew comfort and strength from religious faith, the better his or her chances of survival. Those who did not rely on faith died at a rate three times higher.[1]

The son of a colleague of mine was diagnosed with a very progressive form of cancer. They are devout Christians. The prognosis for the young man was grim. The young man never lost the faith that he would be healed despite the prognosis. His faith community began praying in earnest. After several chemotherapy treatments, there is no sign of the cancer. The doctors are baffled, but family and friends believe that God was the source of the healing. This is not a unique story. There are many, many accounts like this one where medical science is at a loss to explain the recovery of a very ill patient. Faith — the evidence of things not seen.

Knowing self is about understanding the relationship of self to the spirit and the relationship of our spirit to the Almighty Spirit.

Some might question the appropriateness of a discussion of faith in this type of book. We have been taught to keep these types of discussions out of the workplace. While I am a very proud Christian, I am in no way proselytizing. There are many different expressions of faith, not all based on "religion" as we practice it in Western Culture. It is about the belief in a higher source of power that ignites the "fire within" that allows us to press on anyhow — in spite of monumental adversity and barriers. It is about the belief that "troubles don't last always"—that the sun will rise, will set, will rise, will set, will rise, and will set again.

> *Have we not expanded thee thy breast?*
> *And removed from thee thy burden?*
> *So, verily with every difficulty there is relief*
> *Verily with every difficulty there is relief.*
> *Therefore, when thou art free (from thine immediate task), still labor hard,*
> *And to thy Lord turn (all) thy attention.*
>
> The Holy Qur'an, 94th Chapter, Al-Inshirah,
> *Verses 1-2 and 5-8, Yusuf Ali translation*

Spirituality in the Workplace

Spirituality in the workplace is an emerging topic. Recognition that we bring our "whole selves" to work and that it is not possible to offer your best self when suppressing part of your essence has heightened interest in this topic.

Spirituality in the workplace is a very sensitive topic. When we hear the term "spirituality," many immediately think religion. Our democratic values allow for myriad religious and spiritual expressions most everywhere but in the workplace. We dance around the issues of separation of church and state because such topics can become controversial very quickly.

In the past, the common way to deal with such issues in the workplace was to avoid the discussion. We now realize that we find our most creative, intuitive, and innovative selves deep within our spirits. Additionally, in today's faster than fast e-world, increasingly workers need ways to cope better with the pressures of constant change.

Many companies are beginning to recognize that the traditional solutions to workplace stress are inadequate for such tumultuous times. Meditation rooms and spirituality discussion groups are two innovative ways that companies are beginning to address these issues.

As an example, one of my clients, a Fortune 100 company, set up a special room in the middle of a manufacturing complex. Quite a departure from the norm, this area really stood out with wallpaper, a library of self-help and interpersonal support books, relaxing New Age music, and reclining chairs with massage features. At first, employees complained that the company was wasting money that could have been used for raises; but it has become a place for conducting meetings, resolving conflicts, or just taking a time-out from the stresses of the day. These are quiet rooms where you can privately express your faith.

Other companies provide meditation rooms, where employees can go to express their faiths. Acknowledging the "whole" person and his or her needs leads to higher productivity and overall job satisfaction.

The important question is: What can you do as an individual to manage your own workplace angst through your faith?

Center yourself before going to work. Most of us rush out the door in the morning without a moment to spare. I have a friend who puts on her makeup in the car en route to work. Like many, I eat my bagel and drink my coffee while trying to navigate the steering wheel. We start our cell phone conversations during drive time. All of these "got too much to do and too little time to do it" activities add to our stress levels so that by the time we get to work, we are often already in a state of frenzy. Why not use drive time to relax and get centered? Deep breathing exercises, listening to quiet music, praying, or just simply being with yourself in a meditative state can make a big impact on the quality of the rest of your day, not to mention travel safety.

Allocate time for "spirit-spots" throughout the day. Once we get to work, there are the routine projects and then there are the "fires" (the unexpected) to put out. In this fast-paced world of rapid change, there are more "fires" than routine projects these days. In his book The *Future of Success,* Robert Reich, former Secretary of Labor under former President William Clinton, says that most middle income, married couples with children are working about seven weeks longer each year than they did 10 years ago. As individuals, we each work an average of two weeks more each year than we did 20 years ago.[2]

Scheduled breaks are a thing of the past for many of us. We don't even take lunch breaks like we should. So why not take "spirit-spots"? These are 30-second to five-minute mini-breaks where you tune everything out and invoke spirit. Ask yourself: What is going on for me right now? What do I need to do to center myself? No quiet place to go? Try a bathroom stall! Pray, meditate, or recite an affirmation. Do whatever works for you.

As we get older, many of us are returning to the values that were so much a part of our upbringing. Sometimes it seems that it is not until we are in "trouble" that we seek faith solutions. When times are "good" again, we forget that which sustained us during the storm. During the periods of prosperity and peace, it is important to show gratitude for our many blessings.

Affirmation: I will keep faith, even if it is the size of a mustard seed.

Summary of Key Points:

- Faith in a higher source of power helps us to cope in these troubled times.

- Whether or not you are "religious," spirituality can be the answer when nothing else seems to make sense.

- "We see what we believe."

- Spirituality in the workplace is a growing phenomenon as we cope with more pressures.

- Increasingly, there is recognition that we cannot do our best work without bringing our "whole" selves, including the spiritual self, to the workplace.

- Meditation rooms, dialogue groups, and other remedies are growing in popularity in the corporate world.

- You can manage stress in the workplace through expressions of faith, such as prayer, meditation, centering exercises, and "spirit spots."

Ask Yourself:

1. Do I separate my spirituality from my work world?

2. How can I express my faith in the workplace, while respecting others?

3. Do I have faith at least the size of a mustard seed?

Chapter 5
Unleash the Unique You

It is far better to walk fully in your own footprints than a force fit into someone else's.

Jonetta Cole, Presidential Distinguished Professor at
Emory University, President Emerita, Spelman College,
from Dream the Boldest Dreams

Once you know "you," you then have to unleash "you." There are some of us who know ourselves very well, but we still do not open our best selves to the universe.

Sometimes we don't know how to channel, leverage, or optimize our gifts. I knew that I wanted to write and speak. I had finally understood that I had a gift of motivating and inspiring others. Even though it took me a considerable amount of time to come to know in my soul that this was my calling, I still did not know how to unleash it to the world.

When I was asked to speak, I would research the topic, write out my comments word for word, and stand and deliver it word for word. People applauded and gave me positive feedback but there was something missing. After these presentations, I did not feel that I had really given as much as I had to offer. I felt stifled by the written comments, even though I had written them.

I reflected on this for quite a while. If this was my gift, why did it not feel comfortable for me? Why did it feel forced? Stilted? I came to two conclusions. Often I was given the topic that the group wanted to hear about. I did not consider whether I really felt comfortable with the topic or even wanted to speak on that topic. I honored the request and many times would have to do extensive research because I was not an expert on the topic. The second issue was that I really could not settle in on a delivery approach until I had interacted with the audience. I needed to be in tune with the aura of the audience and the atmosphere — assessing the environment through observation, meditation, and reflection during the actual event.

When I finally decided that I would no longer merely accept the topic given to me, and when I finally got the courage to speak more extemporaneously, I was able to unleash from those unknown depths of my soul. Often I don't know what I am going to say next. I amaze myself! Wow! That was provocative, I will think. I always have an outline, however. Speaking extemporaneously does require some preparation. But it simply means no "word-for-word" prepared speech.

Often I am asked to submit an outline of my comments ahead of time. I now say, "I can't do that because I am not sure of the direction in which I am going to take the topic." They say, "Well if you have spoken on this before, you must have an outline." I tell them that every presentation is customized and unique based on my best thinking at the moment. There is awe, wonderment and learning every single minute of the day. If I use the outline from last time, I miss the new wisdom that I did not have last time. I think about it for weeks leading up to a speech and seek break-through thinking (see Chapter 9) by looking for clues in nature and my everyday experiences.

I remember about two years ago, I was asked to give a few opening comments to a group of employees who were involved in a culture change initiative. They needed a boost because things had been pretty rough. I was the second person to speak. I sat there anticipating what I would say. I was getting a bit nervous because nothing provocative was coming to mind. At the last second, I recalled a phrase that I had heard in my early childhood: *"I am what I am and I am all that I am and I'm it."* They were calling me up to the podium. Oh, was this it? It had to be — I had let my mind go and this is what surfaced. Let me tell you about the history of this phrase.

When I was a little girl, my mother listened to a radio minister out of Chicago every Sunday night at midnight. This was a ritual for her, fiddling with dials to get the reception on the old RCA radio from Chicago to Niagara Falls. But he always eventually came in loud and clear and started every broadcast declaring in a luminous voice: "I am what I am and I am all that I am and I am it!" He would repeat it: "I am what I am and I am all that I am and I am it!" In my pre-adolescent mind I thought: "Isn't he arrogant? That's boastful." We were taught to be humble. Now I understand what he meant. He was uniquely made by the Creator, and he had everything he needed. He was unleashing his power to his listening audience. He was not boastful, just very sure of who he was. He articulated a clear purpose in his messages every Sunday night. It was obvious that he had a strong sense of personal mission and vision.

Well, my corporate audience loved the affirmation. Everybody left the session chanting, *"I am what I am and I am all that I am and I'm it!"* It was the beginning of an awakening, a journey of self-discovery based on an assurance that they, each of them, had all that was necessary to achieve their goals. This new powerful sense of self allowed us to have a discussion about personal mission and vision. Without a strong belief in your limitless potential, it is almost impossible to have authentic discourse about personal purpose.

Develop a Personal Mission and Vision

Just like organizations must know their purpose — why they are in business and what they are ultimately striving for — we, too, as individuals must be clear about our own mission or calling in life in order to unleash our power.

What am I about? What is special about me? What is my divine purpose on this earth?

Often those close to us can see something that sets us apart that we cannot see about ourselves. We often take our gifts for granted. I did not know that I had a gift for speaking and writing until others began to point it out. Listen for the clues. How do others describe you? For what kinds of things do you get special compliments? What brings you the greatest joy? What legacy do you want to leave? What do you want your obituary to say?

I participated in an executive development session many years ago. The instructor asked us to write our obituaries. I was under 30 at the time. The first line of the obituary I had written for this exercise read: "Age 99." The instructor asked why I wanted to live to be 99 and I innocently remarked, "I want to live a long time." I did not want to think about my own mortality. I have come to understand in the last 20 years that I cannot control the number of days that I have on this earth, but I can control the quality of each one. I can find and live my purpose, which is inspiring ingenuity in myself and others. I would like my obituary to read:

"She spent every day living her vision of inspiring herself and others to unleash their true potential."

I realize that I am likely not telling you anything that you haven't heard a thousand times before, but have you written a personal mission and vision? Most of us know we need to have a will, but according to a study conducted by FindLaw, a legal Web site, an estimated 59 percent of adults in the United States don't have a will.[1] Additionally, the AARP found that 40 percent of adults over 50 responding to a recent AARP survey didn't have a will.[2] So knowing what you should do and doing it are two different things.

Stop reading right now if you have not written a personal mission and vision. Go work on it and don't pick up this book again until you at least have a draft. Start by thinking about what you would want people to say about you at your funeral. Answer the questions: What is my purpose? Why am I here? For vision, ask yourself: What is my ultimate calling? If I could be doing exactly what I wanted every second of the day, what would it look like?

Putting Others' Opinions in Perspective

Being able to articulate a vision is just the first step. You must begin to live it to unleash your power. That is the hard part, and it becomes your life's work. The beauty, though, is when you get off course, you always have your written mission statement to which you can refer. In the absence of a well-developed personal mission, well...you know the answer to that one. You continue to flounder trying to find your way. It is not easy to stay centered on your path. There will be many obstacles, including well-meaning people in your life with lots of advice. Therefore, the second step to unleashing yourself is to be able to put others' opinions into their proper perspective. Others give us advice from their frame of reference. It can be useful input, but it is not necessarily right for you.

Developing the ability to discern between advice that will support your own mission and vision and that which is nice to know, but you can't use, is paramount in the journey to find self. You will not be able to discern well if you do not have a firmly convicted purpose that you are living.

Some of the well-meaning others may be professional counselors, mentors, or coaches. Counselors typically "advise" people based on a set of facts and information that they have about the individual. Mentors give advice based on their own experiences.

Coaches, on the other hand, promote self-discovery. Counselors and mentors tend to "tell" while coaches "ask." Coaches invite individuals to find their own meaning and answers. In your quest for finding self and developing a personal mission, I recommend seeking the services of a coach in addition to a career counselor or mentor. A coach is trained to be neutral, non-judgmental, and objective.

Do not be overly influenced by what others think about you or what you should do. Learn to appreciate such input, be able to sort out how it fits or doesn't, and stay firm to your own mission. Highly self-differentiated individuals are able to accept input from others without losing their sense of self. Nobody really knows you as well as you know you. Being confident in the knowledge of self—"I am what I am"—is essential in order to unleash.

> *Public opinion is a weak tyrant compared to our own private opinion. What a man thinks of himself, that is what determines, or rather dictates his fate.*
>
> *Henry David Thoreau 19th-Century American Essayist, Poet, and Philosopher*

Self-Assessment Tools Can Help You "Unleash"

There are many ways to foster self-understanding so you can offer your best self to the workplace and the world. Once you know your values and principles, are firmly rooted in what you stand for, and have developed a meaningful purpose, it is time to think in greater depth about your natural ways of being.

There are numerous psychological self-assessment instruments designed to help you understand your natural personality traits, instincts, ways of communicating, leadership styles, and strategies of handling conflict, etc. These aids can be one source of information in your quest for self-understanding but should not be the sole input. They can confirm attributes or bring into sharper focus some gifts that you may not have fully appreciated. They should not be used as crutches or excuses for not developing certain skills or competencies, but they can be very useful in confirming and affirming.

The most popular personality inventory used in the corporate world is the Myers-Briggs Type Indicator (MBTI)®.[3] Based on the work of Swiss psychologist Carl Jung and Americans, Katharine Briggs and Isabel Briggs-Myers, it is designed to uncover your natural preferences on four different dimensions (extrovert/introvert; sensors/intuitives; thinkers/feelers; judgers/perceivers)[4] as outlined in Figure 4.

Figure 4
Myers-Briggs Personality Types

Extroverts (E) OR	Introverts (I)
Have high energy	Have quiet energy
Talk a lot	Talk less
Think out loud	Think before they act
Like to be around people a lot	Are comfortable spending time alone
Are easily distracted	Have good concentration

Sensors (S) OR	Intuitives (N)
Admire practicality	Admire creativity
Focus on the facts and specifics	Focus on ideas and the big picture
Have straightforward speech	Have roundabout thoughts
Are more realistic—see what is	Are more imaginative—see possibilities
Are more present-oriented	Are more future-oriented

Thinkers (T) OR	Feelers (F)
Are cool and reserved	Are warm and friendly
Are objective	Get their feelings hurt easily
Are honest and direct	Are sensitive and diplomatic
Are naturally critical	Try hard to please others
Are motivated by achievement	Are motivated by being appreciated

Judgers (J) OR	Perceivers (P)
Are serious and formal	Are playful and casual
Are time-conscious	Are unaware of time or late
Like to make plans	Like to wait and see
Work first, play later	Play first, work later
Like to finish projects best	Like to start projects best

You may have taken the Myers-Briggs or heard people talk about being an *INTJ* or an *ESFP*.

I am an *ENTJ*. Understanding my "type" has helped me to better interact with people who are my opposites. My partner is an *INFP*. The most conflict arises in our relationship around my *J*-ness. I am very time-conscious and like to make plans. He is not conscious of time and likes to wait and see. I spend a lot of time waiting for him to "show up." While it is frustrating for me, my insistence on "planning" is equally frustrating for him. It is easier to manage the conflict because we understand our behaviors arise from our personality types and not some deliberate attempt to displease one another.

In organizations, such an exercise helps people see how they are different from each other and how those differences can enhance or inhibit teamwork. Surfacing that you are introverted can be a freeing discovery for you personally. You may have already known it intuitively, but having it validated provides a certain sense of acceptance. "I am who I am." For those who lack self-differentiation and want to "copy" or be like someone else, such revelations may cause greater frustration. While there are no right or wrong "types," some of us may tend to put judgments on the various attributes. "I don't want to be an introvert!" was a declaration from someone who had taken the inventory. He viewed "introversion" as a "bad thing," primarily because he felt that it was not a valued attribute in his corporate culture.

The business world needs all types working together towards the common vision. Our strength lies in our diversity and our ability to leverage our unique contributions. As you learn more about yourself, your goal should be to make what is already good, better. Harness, leverage, optimize, develop, highlight, and unleash your gifts!

> *There are two kinds of talents, man-made talent and God-given talent. With man-made talent, you have to work very hard. With God-given talent, you just touch it up once in a while.*
>
> Pearl Bailey, 20th-Century American Singer and Actress

Another psychological self-assessment based on "natural instincts" was developed by Kathy Kolbe (Kolbe A® index) from her research on learning differences among children.[5] It is based on the premise that we each have instinctive ways of being that sometimes are not appreciated, leveraged, or optimized in our work or life. We can be more productive when we allow our instincts to be an integral, deliberate part of our decision processes along with facts, education, discipline, and values.

Kolbe believes, however, that too often education, discipline, and value systems have been used to unnecessarily suffocate instinct. The Kolbe system attempts to bring a complementary balance among learned behaviors and instinct.

There are four Action Modes® in the Kolbe system: *fact-finder* (like to collect data, define terms, establish priorities); *follow-through* (instinctively seek order, work sequentially, establish procedures); *quick start* (take risks, promote experimentation, defy the odds), and *implementors* (create tangible goods, provide physical protection, build hand-crafted models).

My personal instinctive and dominant strength based on the Kolbe system was *quick start*. It means: I am highly instinctive and the advice was to trust my instincts. "When you trust your instinctive talent, not only will you get more done, but the end result will be more effective. This driving force requires taking on challenges, acting on intuition, and embracing open-ended opportunities. Nothing slows you down more than planning ahead or having to justify your instincts. Trust your sense of urgency to 'go for it,' even though you can't be sure of the results."

I could barely contain myself as I read this description. I had chills, goose bumps, and my stomach did flips. "Yes! Yes! This is me. I'm not irresponsible, impulsive (well, maybe sometimes), or just plain unfocused." When I am exposed to a new idea for business or meet a new person, I immediately know when it is right. I am not sure how I know but I just get that strong urge to move on it. Sometimes I declare the outcome at the instant I meet a new person, for example.

When I met my partner, I told a friend within five minutes of our meeting, "He is the one." And he was and is! Even though my Myers-Briggs type suggested that I am time-conscious and like to plan, I don't think the two themes are inconsistent. I like to know my schedule for the day, but it can be subject to change. I don't like not knowing what lies immediately ahead because I do like to be prepared.

Each of us, undoubtedly, has some of each of the attributes outlined in the MBTI and the Kolbe System. We can certainly adapt and learn to use other characteristics as needed. The key is to know where we have our most predominant tendencies, to be proud of them, and to offer them unapologetically to the world.

Throughout my career in the corporate environment I was encouraged to work on my weaknesses. While we all have the ability, through hard work and perseverance, to turn our weaknesses into strengths, it is much more productive to work on enhancing our gifts. As an instinctive *quick start,* I am certainly not perfect. But I can offer so much more to the workplace if I understand some of the pitfalls of my natural style. I sometimes don't listen well because I quickly come to conclusions. I tend to interrupt people because I get so enthusiastic about a new idea. And I get bored easily and show my emotions through gestures and body language. I can and do work on these areas so that I am able to interact more effectively with other people.

I also capitalize on my natural style of making things up as I go rather than having a strategy. I used to worry that I could not easily sit down and plan out a complete strategy. As I stated in Chapter 3, I did not have business plan when I started my business. I just seized opportunities. My advisors saw my inability to plan and stick to it as a major character flaw. I started to feel inadequate. Once I found my passion, though — speaking and writing — I learned to leverage my natural instincts for serendipity and innova-tion. I hired a chief operating officer for the business to handle the planning, fact-finding, and follow-through. Rather than try to build competencies· in areas that are not my natural instinctive strengths, I found someone who naturally possesses the complementary skills.

I would be unproductive to the point of dysfunction if I was forced to function outside of my instinctive style. It is counter-productive for organizations to expend resources trying to teach people how to "fit" molds that are not natural for them. As I stated in Chapter 3, I spent 11 years in corporate America trying to fit in. Corporate America rewarded fact-finders and follow-through types—two instincts that are very low for me.

Organizations need some of each type. *Quick starts* foster creativity, help alleviate "analysis paralysis," and are natural risk-takers. Many traditional companies are not able to keep pace with the need for fast turnaround and innovation, because of past practices during the industrial era of hiring and promoting primarily *fact-finders, implementors,* and *follow-through* types. I was certainly a "misfit" in the corporate environment not only because of my race and gender but because of my instinctive *quick start* style. I had three strikes! No wonder I felt compelled to leave!

I tried desperately to fit in, but the depth of the conflict caused me to come to blows with myself—my head and my heart had it out! My head said: "But you make good money and have done well by others' standards. You are the first in your family to have this kind of opportunity. This is what the civil rights struggle was about. What did you fight for?" But my heart was crying out: "This is not you. There is so much more...just listen and let me out."

In the end, the heart won and I was unleashed in search of myself.

Remember always that you not only have the right to be an individual, you have an obligation to be one. You cannot make any useful contribution unless you do this.

Eleanor Roosevelt

Affirmation: I will unleash my natural gifts and work on strengthening, leveraging, and optimizing them. I will honor my special gifts and offer them to the universe.

Summary of Key Points:

- Even when we know our gifts, we sometimes do not know how to unleash them.

- "I am what I am and I am all that I am and I am it!" is a powerful affirmation to provide the assurance that each of us has everything we need to achieve our vision.

- A personal mission statement is critical to self-understanding and unleashing your unique gifts.

- As you unleash your gifts, put others' opinions in their proper perspective.

- Psychological self-assessment tools can be useful in validating and affirming your natural way of being.

- Work on enhancing your strengths rather than improving on your weaknesses.

Ask Yourself:

1. Do I know what my gifts are?

2. Have I unleashed my gifts? Do I know how?

3. Am I unduly influenced by others' opinions?

4. Do I believe, "I am what I am and I am all that I am and I am it"?

5. Do I have a personal mission statement? Do I have a vision for my life?

6. Have I explored my natural ways of being through self-assessment instruments?

7. Do I work on enhancing my strengths or am I more focused on improving on my weaknesses?

Chapter 6
Know Your Natural Response to Change

To act and act wisely when the time for action comes,
to wait and wait patiently when it is time for repose,
put man in accord with the rising and falling of tides,
so that with nature and law at his back,
and truth and beneficence as his beacon light,
he may accomplish wonders.
Ignorance of this law results in periods of
unreasoned enthusiasm on the one hand, and
depression on the other.
Man thus becomes the victim of the tides when he
should be their Master.

Helean Petrova Blavatsky,
19th-Century Russian Writer and Theosophist

As you grow in self-enlightenment, so will your awareness of your natural response mechanisms. We are each different, with a different history and culture—it all makes us who we are. As pointed out in the last chapter, some are extroverts, others introverts. Some are *quick starts,* others *fact-finders.* Some are liberals, others conservatives. We have natural ways in which we respond to conflict—natural ways in which we each respond to change. Understanding your natural way of handling change is the first step in taking responsibility for managing change.

The rate of change is faster than it has ever been in any time in our history. More new information has been acquired in the last 50 years than in all of history. Technology is advancing at rates that create a feeling of never being able to stay current or know everything that we need to know— new software to learn, new concepts to digest, and new information to obtain from the Internet.

Cultural anthropologists say that, biologically, baby boomers are not equipped to handle the rate of change that we are experiencing. The chaos and feeling of being totally out of control comes with the revolutionary transformation that we are experiencing. It is too much for our metabolisms, which are wired for a more evolutionary rate of change.

> *Man has a limited biological capacity for change. When this capacity is overwhelmed, the capacity is in future shock.*
>
> *Alvin Toffler*

We see the manifestation of this in new and scary phenomena like "road rage," workplace violence, and "airplane rage." A growing problem with people who are not able to handle the instability in the workplace and literally lose control has been dubbed "going postal." It seems that very often we read of a new episode of a disgruntled worker tragically killing or wounding bosses and co-workers. It is such a problem that training sessions are very common to help managers and other employees deal with workplace violence. According to the U.S. Bureau of Labor Statistics, workplace violence, including assaults and suicides, accounted for 16 percent of all work-related fatal occupational injuries in 2000. Violent acts are consistently named among the top three causes of workplace fatalities for all workers.[1]

In all of this turmoil and chaos, we need to understand our individual response to change. Some of us have experienced a great deal of change in our lives—perhaps we moved frequently during childhood, or maybe we had an unstable family environment with different adult caretakers. Perhaps

147

change was commonplace for you as you developed into adulthood. If this is the case, you may be better able to cope with the instability that we now have in the workplace. On the other hand, if your developmental years were characterized by little change — a more routine existence where you lived in the same house with the traditional family unit intact and where your job situation was stable with most of your career with one employer — then you may have a more difficult time addressing the magnitude of change we are experiencing today.

Based on research we have conducted with over 9,000 employees, I have formulated six "types" of employee reactions to the changing workplace. I call them the six *F's* (see Figure 5). I invite you to be honest with yourself and identify where you think you fit along this continuum. Have fun with this. It is not intended to label you because we probably all have some of each type, but rather to raise awareness of how many of us handle change.

Figure 5

THE SIX F'S
Responses to Change

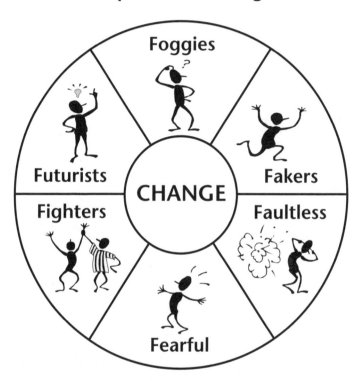

Type 1: The "Foggies." I estimate this to be about 10 percent of the workforce. They are in a "fog," so to speak. This group has either been in a protected, stable environment not impacted by change or simply chooses to ignore change. These individuals stand firm and unmovable. The "protected group" is very comfortable, may have read about the issues of the changing workplace, but can't see how it would ever apply to them. A representative comment from a *foggy* in an industry that has become highly competitive is: "I think all of the talk about competition is overstated. I haven't seen any increase in competition in the 25 years that I have been here." When he made this statement in a focus group, everyone else looked at him in disbelief as if to say, "Where have you been?" My answer: "In a fog." Those who ignore change are sometimes left alone in the organization, in their own little world. "Well you know Sally, she is going to do it her way until she retires. We just work around her."

Foggies are oblivious or choose to ignore change, and their circumstances may allow them to do so more easily than others. It is dangerous to remain in this state, even if there is no foreseeable change in your field. Staying current with what is happening around you and knowing what you would do in the event of a significant change is what I call an "I'm ready" mindset in Chapter 10.

> *Notice that the stiffest tree is most easily cracked, while the bamboo or willow survives by bending with the wind.*
>
> Bruce Lee, 20th-Century American Actor and Martial Artist

Type 2: The "Fakers." They try to convince others and often themselves that they are with the "change program." They know the words to say and "pay lip service" to management, but deep down inside, they have no intention of changing their behavior because they hope that this, too, shall pass and everything will return to "normal." Another reason that many *fakers* do not change is because they do not know how to, but are afraid to admit that they are having difficulty managing change. We need to take a close look at ourselves and ask, "Am I faking it? Am I really going through internal turmoil and stress but putting on a 'happy face'?"

The response to change messages can fall into three patterns for *fakers:*

1. "I heard the words but this, too, shall pass. It is just another program of the month. I will just wait it out. There's no need to do anything differently, but I won't be too conspicuous or vocal. They are so busy trying to implement this change, that I won't be noticed. By the time they notice me, they will be on to the next 'new thing.'"

2. "I heard the words and understand intellectually. This really is a message for others, not me. I already know this stuff. I hope all of those others get with the program."

3. "I heard the words . . . understand intellectually . . . I know what I have to do to change." (The new behavior doesn't happen. These individuals may have even convinced themselves they are changing.)

The issue for *fakers* is they do not internalize the change message by grappling with how they feel about it and what they must do personally to make the mental, "gut-level" connection.

> **You will suddenly realize that the reason you did not change before, is because you did not want to.**
>
> Robert Schuller, Contemporary Clergyman,
> Author and Founder of the Crystal Cathedral

Type 3: The "Faultless." They see the changes around them, do not like them, and constantly complain. They see themselves as hopeless victims of an unfair system. This group believes they are entitled to their jobs, increased benefits, and annual raises. They believe that they have done everything right, their plight is beyond their control, and someone else is to blame. If the business results are not adequate, it is obviously management's fault. A *faultless* employee might say: "If we just had better leadership, everything would be okay" or "I have been a good employee for 25 years, and this is not fair."

It may be true that many in the workplace today are *faultless*. So what? It doesn't help to change anything by simply attributing the blame elsewhere for others to "fix." We must move to a model of shared responsibility. First, accept that there is no one individual or group of people (e.g., the government, leadership) to blame for the metamorphosis we are going through. Then, assess your own situation, how you are responding, and take personal responsibility for solutions. See what your role is in the change equation. Leadership has a role to play, but individual contributors do as well. In the industrial era command-and-control model, most individual contributors looked to management to "fix" things and be responsible for ensuring our well-being. That model simply does not work anymore. In a world where there are more questions than absolutes, leadership does not hold the key to the puzzle.

> *You must be the change you wish to see in the world.*
>
> *Mahatma Gandhi, 20th-Century Leader of
> Indian Nationalism and a Prophet of Nonviolence*

Recognize that the solutions are complex with the magnitude of change we are experiencing, and each of us has a role to play.

There may be more of a tendency in the *faultless* phase for a psychological concept known as Attribution Theory and the fundamental attribution error.[2] In Western culture, we tend to attribute positive intent to things that we do and negative intent to others. We attribute our own behavior to the situation at hand, but for others it is because of their dispositions or makeup. As an example, we would label leaders as the problem in general, not based on a given situation but because "leadership is like that."

I concur with the popular psychological theories that our judgments about other people are weighted averages of the information we have about them. We tend to take everything we know about them — giving negative information greater weight. Therefore, it is normal, especially in the wake of difficult chaotic change, to focus on the negative even more.

> **Whatever one of us blames in another, each will find in his own heart.**
>
> *Seneca*

The *faultless* also tend to critique the process instead of the outcome. I was reading some chat room e-mail on the Internet, written by people who have been impacted by the 2002 round of job cuts. They talked about how unfair it was to be literally walked out the door or about the poor choice of words that the manager used to tell them they had been fired. Another focused on "his ideas" and hard work that had gone unappreciated. While all of these claims may be absolutely correct, lamenting the unfairness of the situation will do little to alter it. Anger, blame, and denial are natural reactions to "loss." Being aware of these normal reactions will help you to work through these stages so that you can move on to questioning yourself: "How am I functioning? What is my personal responsibility for managing the next steps of my life? What is my plan?"

Type 4: The "Fearful." The events of the past 15 years have left many of us in a state of constant fear. Nobody wants to lose their job or hear that their job is no longer secure. Uncertainty could mean not being able to meet personal financial obligations. And if you are a typical baby boomer who got trapped in the material acquirement spiral, you really do need your job. Fear is a natural response to uncertainty when there is so much at stake.

Fearful people engage in self-protectionist, non-team-oriented behavior. There is low trust, and oftentimes paranoia sets in. *Fearful* people are not as productive because they are busy trying to protect themselves from an undesirable fate, such as the loss of their jobs. They hang onto every word from the rumor mill and try to do exactly what they think the boss wants. Every action is analyzed and scrutinized for some underlying meaning. They are very cautious and play it "close to the vest," so to speak. They are very rarely successful because the behavior that emanates from fear often leads to the very eventuality feared most—loss of job.

> *Whenever we're afraid, it's because we don't know enough. If we understood enough, we would never be afraid.*
>
> Earl Nightingale, Contemporary American Motivational Speaker and Co-founder of Nightingale-Conant Corp.

It is not easy to deal with fear because we live in fear-inducing times. What can you do to manage the fear that an uncertain job future can bring? First, "name it and claim it." Awareness is always the first step. Next, decide what you are going to do about it. Do you need professional help? If you decide "no," then what are you going to do to handle the challenges of the workplace so that you can function in a positive way? You will certainly need all of your coping skills—all the knowledge, experience, optimistic outlook, and self-help savvy that you can muster.

Some effective techniques for managing fear include:

- Taking responsibility for planning a way to cope
- Taking rational and composed action rather than reacting impulsively
- Seeking advice and support
- Looking for something positive to come from the struggle (e.g., learning)
- Staying confident
- Using humor

Ineffective techniques are:

- Being hostile and confrontational
- Publicly venting strong feelings
- Blaming self or others
- Not being able to make decisions
- Ignoring or downplaying the problem
- Suppressing emotions by keeping feelings to yourself
- Giving up trying
- Escaping (e.g., compulsive behavior such as overeating, drinking, etc.)

Coping with fear-inducing situations is a process, but it does not come easily for anyone. It requires you to learn about specific ways of coping and to understand which ones work for you. The key is to do something—something active and positive to address your fears.

Ask yourself, "What am I most afraid of? The loss of this job? The thought of having to look for another job? That my skills are not up to speed? That I will be targeted for layoff simply because I don't get along with the boss?" Once you know the real source of fear, it is easier to know what to do about it.

> *Our deepest fear is not that we are inadequate. Our deepest fear is that we are powerful beyond measure. It is light, not our darkness that frightens us most.*
>
> *Nelson Mandela, Former President of the Republic of South Africa*

Type 5: The "Fighters" (for status quo or change). The *fighters* for status quo are typically long-service employees who have gained the respect of co-workers and managers. They have a great deal of history in the organization and openly share their knowledge. They cling to tradition with all of their might. A status quo *fighter* might say: "We tried that 25 years ago and it did not work, so I don't think we ought to attempt it again."

Status quo *fighters* also engage in covert activities to ensure that little change occurs. They lobby quietly behind the scenes in ways that often go undetected as being anti-change. Their arguments are often compelling, and they choose their opportunities carefully so as not to raise suspicion. For example, status quo *fighters* would probably not be very vocal in a meeting on change. (May take a *faker* stance.) They would wait until the meeting was over and seek opportunities to persuade others to their point of view.

The second type of *fighter* wants change and feels frustrated by the lack of progress. They are vanguards, often seen as troublemakers. These change "warriors" are not always so tactful and sometimes attempt to browbeat co-workers into changing. In very strong traditional cultures, "warriors" are often "rejected" because of their "warrior" ideas and tactics. In one of the organizations in which we consult, "warriors" are being hired because the company realizes that it needs people who are willing to challenge the culture. The old status quo culture, however, is so entrenched that the majority of these change advocates leave the company frustrated after a short period of time.

Change advocates do exactly what they have been asked to do, but there is so much resistance, that their efforts are often punished rather than rewarded. They are told by the "old guard" that they are moving too quickly, and the system cannot take such radical change all at once. They often have little support in the organization; and sometimes, the very people who hired them end up turning their backs on them when the pressure is too much.

> *Most people guard against going into the fire, and so end up in it.*
>
> *Rumi*

Type 6: The "Futurists." This group may comprise 25 percent of the workforce. They may be GenXers or GenYers — individuals accustomed to change, and/or highly self-differentiated, or workers new to the culture. They are adaptable, flexible, and global in their thinking. They know that they are in control of their destinies. They are career-resilient. They have a high self-concept and resist laying blame when things don't turn out as they would have liked. They get up, dust themselves off from the fall, and forge ahead. *Futurists* are not fearful because they believe in themselves and have a plan *B* and maybe even a plan *C*. They are highly successful in anything that they attempt because of their determination and optimistic outlook.

Futurists know themselves well, are physically fit, have high energy, and are genuinely open to new ideas. They are experimenters and are not afraid of making mistakes. They understand that trial and error over and over again is the only way to make progress. They are well-read, stay ahead of the curve, and take personal risks, fully accepting the consequences. They view failures as learning experiences and move on without losing much ground.

163

Futurists are not perfect by any stretch of the imagination. They tend to be impulsive, relying almost totally on intuition rather than fact. Many are *quick starts* as described in Chapter 5. They may be impatient and sometimes literally burn themselves out trying to keep many "balls in the air." Some have not learned to calibrate their "speed" and "spin out of control." But when they find the right balance and perspective, the *futurists* succeed in highly changeable environments.

> **No pessimist ever discovered the secrets of the stars, nor sailed an uncharted land, or opened a new haven to the human spirit.**
>
> Helen Keller, 20th-Century American
> Visually- and Hearing-Impaired Author, Lecturer

What is Your Natural Response to Change?

Actually, we all probably have a little bit of each category in us. To some extent we all want to ignore the changes around us, especially if we are comfortable where we are *(foggies)*. We have all tried to go along with the program, even if we didn't fully understand exactly what was happening *(fakers)*. It is only human nature to think, "it's not my fault" when it truly isn't *(faultless)*. We have all fought for things that we believed in *(fighters)*, and we have behaved like futurists at some point in our careers.

Moving forward, it is not right or wrong to be in any of the stages at any given time, but understanding where you are helps you to know if you think you would be better off adopting a different mindset about change. It may be appropriate for you to ignore change sometimes or to fake it. As long as you are aware of your state of being at any time, you are likely going to do a better job of managing the change. Ultimately, however, you will be better off moving towards the *futurist* type. This is a difficult journey for some of us. As always, the first step is to become aware of your current state, and how far that is from where you want to be. Then, examine the steps that it will take to get there.

Affirmation: I will understand my personal response to change. I will work on managing and eliminating attitudes which will inhibit me from embracing change and being in control of my own destiny.

Summary of Key Points:

- Everybody responds to change differently.

- Understanding your natural response to change can help you better manage change.

- It is only natural to resist change in one way or another.

- The healthiest response to change is that of the *futurist,* who believes in himself or herself and always has an alternate course of action.

Ask Yourself:

1. What do the changes in my workplace mean for me personally?

2. How am I handling the change emotionally?

3. What must I do to succeed in this new work environment?

4. What will it look like when I am in this new state?

5. What will I be doing differently?

6. What are the steps that I must take along the way?

7. Do I believe that one person or set of managers is responsible for all the turmoil in my job, in my field?

8. Am I confident that I can be a part of changing things for the better?

Chapter 7

Learn to Be at Peace with the Paradoxes of Change

Change means movement. Movement means friction.
Only in a frictionless vacuum of a non-existent abstract
world can movement or change occur without that
abrasive friction of conflict.

Saul Alinsky, 20th-Century Social Activist

Once you have come to greater self-awareness and understand your natural response to change, it will be easier to
accept the paradoxes of change. But still, one of the reasons
that change is so difficult is that it puts us in a quandary.
We feel a sense of conflict. Change causes confusion. We
are often torn between two belief systems—two or more
paradigms. We want to reduce the uncertainty of our
choices, but the magnitude of the change we are experiencing in the workplace and the world today leaves us with
high levels of uncertainty. There are often no clear answers.
Every avenue seems risky.

> *One may not reach the dawn, save by the path of the night.*
>
> *Kahlil Gibran*

The upheaval in the workplace is real. The chaos in our world is real. Baby boomers who were comfortable and complacent now understand that nothing is certain, and tomorrow is not promised. But still, baby boomers don't like change and why should they? Life was pretty good for most of us, relatively speaking, for several decades after World War II.

Our frame of reference has been stability, financial and material comfort, and an overall sense of predictability and security. We had the sense of comfort of a dry baby's bottom. We liked change as long as we could control it. Like a baby cries out when he or she needs changing, we could control to some extent the amount of change in our lives. Jobs were plentiful and secure, and they were paying enough to allow a very comfortable existence.

This is no more. As we attempt to deal with just the changes in the workplace, we are faced with numerous puzzling paradoxes.

These paradoxes come from the imbalance that arises when we have one foot firmly planted in the old industrial-age thinking and the other teetering in the new era. There are many sacred assumptions that we cling to even though they no longer hold up in the new environment. There are processes and practices that keep us from being as productive as we could be, but we will not discontinue because of a fear of letting go of what is familiar and comfortable.

During these times of monumental transition, it is only natural to feel imbalanced. We get mixed signals, which are frustrating and can cause a great deal of stress. I invite you to look at change differently and explore these seeming dichotomies with a new attitude — one of acceptance and openness. These new attitudes can be the foundation of your success in the 21st century. They can even help you understand yourself.

> *In every crisis there is a message. Crises are nature's way of forcing change . . . breaking down old structures, shaking loose negative habits so that something new and better can take its place.*
>
> Susan Taylor, Contemporary Author and
> Editorial Director of ESSENCE Magazine

Here are some examples:

Paradox #1: Simultaneously, be a specialist and be multiskilled.

What happened to the day when we could simply concentrate on our specialty? If you were an accountant, you didn't need to understand the principles of total quality management or how to lead a meeting. If you were a nurse, you didn't have to understand issues of health-care reimbursement. If you were a teacher, you were not also required to be a social worker.

Most baby boomers have been in the workplace for enough years to be specialists at something. Even if it is not your calling or your passion work, it is something that you are comfortable doing because it is how you earn a living.

But suddenly your specialty is not good enough. Your employer now demands that you learn new skills. It could be computers, group facilitation, teamwork, intercultural communication, or any number of other competencies.

I can't tell you the number of baby boomers in the corporate world who have told me that they just want to be left alone to do their jobs. They are not interested in learning a bunch of new "stuff." They are too old and they think they probably will retire in the next few years anyway.

Many people resist new skills training. Resistance usually comes from fear that we will not be able to learn new skills. Fear will prevail until you find the courage to take the first step. That first step is so gratifying. It feels good to accomplish a goal you never dreamed possible. I can't give you the courage to take the first step; you've got to find it on your own. But rest assured you have it, even if it is buried deep within.

The 21st century mandates we keep learning because there is so much more to know, experience, and be as technology advances and the world becomes "smaller." We still need to be specialists, but we also need to learn to be proficient in a number of other areas, some still undefined. It may seem like a paradox — an impossible one at that. It is doable.

"But how?" you ask. It is not that easy. Start small. Sign up for a class in something that you know will help you at work even if you think you don't have the time. Invite a co-worker from another culture to have lunch to learn more about him or her. Write a letter to your local politician offering your opinion about something you feel strongly about. Volunteer to help in a community effort. There is no one right answer. Just promise yourself that, once a month, you will do something that you have never done before or never thought you would do as a means of learning new skills.

Embrace the unknown.

Paradox #2: Just the facts please—but wait, what does your "gut" tell you?

"Management by facts," "root cause analysis," and "data-driven approaches" are popular business phrases. But increasingly today, there is a recognition that the "facts" may not tell the whole story—that we need to expand our definition of the "facts." There is new appreciation for intuitive leadership and decision making. A paradox? At first blush, it might appear to be. The two ideas seem as different as night and day.

The mind (or the head) uses logic, facts, knowledge, tangibles, and observation to come to conclusions. Sometimes we act from our feeling place, which is dangerous because feelings (e.g., anger, frustration, happiness) are temporary. When we act out of feeling, we are being influenced by our current sense of well-being. Operating from intuition is deeper and incorporates our knowledge, experience, values and world-view. We are operating from the enlightened self, from the place that we can rarely explain. That is why it is hard to accept intuition as a valid approach to business problems. We cannot prove our decision is right. It is not backed by data. It is riskier. What if your "gut" is wrong? There is no place to backtrack to see where you made your intuitive mistake. With data, you can retrace your steps to see where the faulty analysis is and fix it. You fix intuition by adding the experience to your wisdom base, but you still can't be sure that next time you will be right.

> *There is a world of difference between truth and facts. Facts can obscure the truth.*
>
> *Maya Angelou, Contemporary American Poet,*
> *Educator, and Actress*

It is not either/or. It is both/and. Fact vs. intuition is only a paradox if you view it as either/or. Certainly, we want to continue to "use our heads" and be in tune with how we feel at any given moment. But in an uncertain world where even the facts are changing daily, a strong intuitive ability is needed. And guess what? You cannot develop your intuitive skills if you do not know yourself well. What will be most critical for success in the new millennium is getting to know ourselves to the depths of our souls—constantly asking: "Who am I? Why am I? What do I stand for? What does my heart know?" We have, up until now, primarily used our head and feelings to make decisions. In a business setting, it was not acceptable to say, "My 'gut' tells me" or "I know in my heart." We have to have a well-developed "gut" in order to use it effectively. It is a journey, my friends—a journey of self-discovery and understanding. Self-knowledge is one of the key business attributes of the 21st century.

When I left corporate America, my head kept telling me that it was a very risky proposition. My experience then led to a range of feelings—from anger to frustration to disappointment to sadness to encouragement and everything else in between. I finally decided to get in tune with my inner being.

I took time to do some soul-searching—to find a quiet place where I could be with myself to think about who I really was and what I really wanted from life. At that juncture, I knew that I could not be my true, authentic self in the corporate environment in which I worked. It was only after the revelation came that I could never know who I was if I kept trying to be somebody else, that I was ready to let my heart lead the way.

Good personal decisions and good business decisions are possible only when all three — the head, the emotions, and the heart — are allowed to enter the picture. We need to let the heart lead much more than we have in the past. We need to be able to feel comfortable saying, "I don't know why I know this, I just do. I know it because my heart has told me."

> *It seems that to find the real path we have to go off the path we are on now, even for an instant, and earn the privilege of losing our way. As the path fades we are forced to take a good look at the life in which we actually find ourselves. For many professionals in the corporate world, going off the path may simply mean approaching work in a more contemplative way, that is, to meditate on work's problems as much with the heart as with the mind.*
>
> *David Whyte*

Listen to your heart.

Paradox #3: Workers have been "empowered" but, you ask: "Where is the power?"

Business messages talk about taking risks — pushing the envelope — "thinking outside the box." But when we do, we are not always rewarded; the consequence may sometimes feel much more like a "punishment." Therein lies the paradox. A crucial aspect of the transition we are in is from a mindset of command and control to that of shared power. This is a difficult shift because most institutions have deep cultural roots tied to a model of hierarchy. We've been conditioned to think about the workplace as comprised of two major groups: workers and bosses. One tells the other what to do and expects compliance without question.

But we have said that the rules have changed. We want a more participatory environment where the distinctions between bosses and workers are less formal. We have set up self-directed and empowered work teams. We said we want to push decision making down so that the people closest to the customer, or those on the "firing line," are not thwarted by layers of bureaucracy.

The confusion results because we are caught in the transition between two models. This is a particularly difficult shift for many of us to make because it requires a mindset shift to a shared power model. It shifts power to those with the knowledge, not just those with the title. It will take society a very long time to learn how to share power.

> *If you pick the right people and give them the opportunity to spread their wings... you almost don't have to manage them.*
>
> Jack Welch

You can help this transition by stepping up to the challenge of leadership. Whether you are a waiter, a grocery store checker, a temporary contract worker, a geologist, or an administrative assistant, you can influence the amount of power you have over your work.

You can determine the extent to which you simply do the right thing on behalf of a customer. You determine if you will make the decision to enhance the look of a report without asking permission. You determine if you will go to the boss with a new suggestion, even though you fear he or she will dismiss it. You determine your tenacity to keep introducing new ideas. And, ultimately, you control the passion that you bring to your work. Even though your attempts to be self-directed and more empowered may be frustrating, don't give up. Understand that a good deal of the frustration results from the fact that society has not fully internalized these different management philosophies.

I am reminded of the story of a woman who participated in a focus group conducted on behalf of her company to better understand employee concerns. She said that she was having a dispute with a co-worker, and her boss told her to go work it out because she was "empowered." She said she would be happy to, but that she lacked the tools. She had never been trained in conflict resolution, for example. I applaud her for recognizing that she needed a new and different skill set. The real power was in her knowledge that she needed to know more to address the situation.

Don't wait for somebody to empower you. Nobody can "empower" us. Empowerment is really a state of mind that comes from within. We hold the power of choice and if we just believe that (believing it is the hard part), then nobody else needs to declare us "empowered." It is easier to embrace empowerment when we know ourselves well and have a clear sense of our purpose.

> *Few people during their lifetime come anywhere near exhausting the resources dwelling within them. There are deep wells of strength that are never used.*
>
> Richard E. Byrd, 20th-Century American Explorer, Author, and Aviator

All power resides within.

Paradox #4: Most organizations claim to value diversity, but conformity is rewarded.

Intuitively, most of us believe that diverse opinions and perspectives can lead to better solutions, but it is tempting to make decisions in isolation for the sake of efficiency. In some ways, the team concept can slow down decision making.

When we bring diverse ideas together, it takes more churning of different thoughts to come to a consensus. In the hierarchical model, fewer people were at the decision-making table so decisions could be made more expediently. Now that we encourage broad input and team decision making, it may seem that diversity actually gets in the way of productivity.

I have served on a number of nominating committees for not-for-profit organizations. Invariably, when the time comes to select new board members, someone will say, "We want to make sure they fit." To me, that is code for: "We want to make sure they think like us."

When I interview managers about the type of people they want on their teams, in one breath they will say diversity is important and in the very next, they will extol the virtues of those individuals who are "team players," easy to manage, and results-oriented. "Team player" is often code for "they think like me."

I have only encountered one really enlightened manager

who knew himself very well, had a high level of self-differentiation, and actively recruited people who had different philosophies from himself. He was the CEO of a not-for-profit foundation. I was interviewing him about his thoughts on diversity and inclusion. He said that when people he interviews express similar ideologies to his own, he will not hire them. In addition, if he believes that their world-view is too aligned with others on his team, he continues his search to ensure the maximum amount of diversity of thought.

This CEO said that this approach has also led to a very racial, ethnic, and gender diverse staff as well. He readily admits that there is increased conflict, and it takes longer to reach closure on issues, but he thinks it is worth all of the extra time because the quality of the result is superior. It has led to extremely innovative ideas for the development of community projects and to funding a number of non-traditional programs.

If you have walked with yourself and been brave enough to

unleash your unique gifts, it will be natural for you to offer your distinctive perspectives, even if they are not accepted by others on the team. Highly self-differentiated people are creative in their attempts to be heard. Criticism or rejection does not deter them. They understand that ideas need to add value. In the end if their solution is not adopted, they objectively discern whether they can support the final decision. Remember that it often takes time to convince others of the value of new ways. Many of our most revered inventors—the Wright Brothers and Alexander Graham Bell, for instance—were initially considered "kooks."

Being "different" was not a good thing in the industrial-era workplace, and it still conjures up images of "weird." If someone says, "I know Fred. He is different," it usually does not paint a positive picture. If we each had the courage to be ourselves, we would have the maximum amount of difference in the world because each of us is unique. Our strength lies in the synergy of bringing together all of our differences.

As we understand the paradoxes of change, knowing the

right balance between conformity and diversity is key. The tendency for homeostasis is so strong that it pulls us back to what is comfortable, what we know. Resist that tendency and stay strong in your resolve to always bring your best self to the workplace—your unique self.

> *Be brave enough to live creatively. The creative is the place where no one else has ever been. You have to leave the city of your comfort and go into the wilderness of your intuition. You cannot get there by bus, only by hard work, risking and by not quite knowing what you are doing. What you will discover will be wonderful: yourself.*
>
> Alan Alda, Contemporary Actor, Writer, and Director

Dare to be you.

Paradox #5: Do more with less.

Now, that is a paradox if we have ever heard one. We continue to receive a clear message in business that we have to learn to do it better, faster, and cheaper with fewer resources—human, financial, and capital. Many of us have probably felt like we are close to the breaking point, with long stressful hours, weekends, and overtime, trying to achieve what seem to be unachievable goals. Competitive pressures necessitate that companies continue to find ways to cut costs and enhance quality. The concept of continuous improvement is here to stay. In order to meet the challenges of changing technology, organizations cannot become complacent, even for a moment.

Advancing technology actually allows us to do more with less, but with one foot in the inefficient old world, and the other foot in the confusing new world, we actually feel less productive. Until we completely abandon the old ways of work in favor of the efficiencies that technology brings, this paradox will continue to cause us anxiety.

As an example, in conducting some research for a major company on how to get closer to the customer, I discovered that all of the sales representatives had laptops and were able to download orders directly to the regional office. The company, however, continued to require the sales representatives to complete a three-part, two-page paper form, with signatures from the customer and the head of sales, before the order would be expedited. When I asked why the paper form was still used, I was given all sorts of convoluted answers, but I concluded that there was simply a fear of letting go of what was familiar and predictable.

We stay stuck in old ways sometimes because we do not have a clear vision of what something different really looks like. The ability to "see" a new way and get passionate about making it a reality will be the key to freeing ourselves from outmoded methods. We must believe that there is always an easier, better, and more efficient way. We are infinitely creative beings when we free our minds from the shackles of the past. The transition period from one method to another may make it seem as if we are working harder, but when we can "see the other side," our passion intensifies and we gain the momentum to reach the new vision.

> **There is a better way.**
>
> *Thomas Edison, 20th-Century American Inventor*

Doing more with less is about letting go emotionally.

Paradox #6: Slow down and move faster.

I see two seemingly inconsistent themes emerging in the work world. One says that we need to find balance between our work and personal lives, and the other is characterized by a greater demand for our time at work. Most of my friends and associates are working longer hours and are feeling pressured to get more done, faster. In my own consulting practice, I notice that there is an increased sense of urgency among my clients to complete projects on a shorter time schedule. The competitive pressures force us to continuously find ways to reduce cycle time and get products to the market faster.

> *We have no simple problems or easy decisions after kindergarten.*
>
> Jack Welch

But there is also a movement we baby boomers are beginning to embrace, which is to slow down, take time to "smell the roses," get in touch with our spirituality, and take sabbaticals for personal renewal and growth. This trend is called "downshifting." There is a significant minority of workers who are leaving high-paying corporate jobs in favor of simpler, slower paced lives.

Some enlightened companies offer paid sabbaticals for their employees to seek renewal and rejuvenation. There are accounts of people taking advantage of this time to do volunteer work or to retool skill sets.

There are thousands of accounts of people who made a conscious choice to calibrate the speed of their lives. They totally changed professions or blended two seemingly un-related fields.

If you love what you do and do only what you love, the balance already exists. As a business owner, I "work" 70 to 80 hours a week; but because it is my passion, it is not "work" by the traditional definition. I rise at 4:30 every morning to write, cook meals, develop client proposals, e-mail my children at college, etc. There is a natural blending of my tasks and activities. I love Caribbean vacations. I often take my laptop, sit on the balcony overlooking the ocean, and write or work on business proposals. Some of my friends think I am crazy and totally out of balance. I find it exhilarating, motivating, and uplifting. I still have time for things like chairing women's day at my church, participating in a book club with friends, and going to movies. When you are engaged in passion work (see Chapter 8), somehow it seems that you have more time to do everything you want to do.

It is more about blending than it is about balancing your work and personal life in the knowledge era. Great new ideas won't always emerge from the traditional 9-5 workday. I keep my home computer in the kitchen because, for some reason, cooking inspires my creativity. Blending comes naturally when you are following your passion.

Finding the right "speed" will be a constant challenge in the 21st century. Technology will continue to allow us to move faster, but just like bigger is not always better, faster is not necessarily always more productive. Moving too fast can lead to disaster. Everybody has his or her own "speed limit"—the speed where you can be your best self. Do you know what yours is?

> *You have the need and the right to spend part of your life caring for your soul...you have to resist the demands of the work-oriented, often defensive element in your psyche that measures life only in terms of output...how much you produce...not in terms of the quality of your life experience.*
>
> *Jean Shinoda Bolen, M.D., Contemporary Internationally Known Lecturer and Author, from her essay, "Windows of the Soul"*

Learn to calibrate your life's speedometer.

There are many more seeming paradoxes that confront you in the workplace—new ones arriving each day as we navigate through the new era.

Recognizing the paradoxes as part of the collision of the two worlds—industrial and knowledge—can make them easier to handle. Not reacting but responding with the knowledge that this is a normal part of change will lessen the anxiety. Understanding that you don't need to have all of the answers—that, in fact, there should be more questions than answers—will give you some peace of mind.

> *A bird does not sing because he has an answer; it sings because it has a song.*
>
> *Maya Angelou*

The increasing complexity of the world makes it imperative that we learn new coping skills. We cannot begin without looking at ourselves and getting in tune with who we really are—what we stand for, what we want from life, and what we give to life. Such introspection takes us to a higher plane of existence and allows us to continually reframe ourselves in the wake of the changes all around us.

Confusion is the welcome mat to the door of creativity.
Michael Gelb, 20th-Century American Motivational Speaker

The power to face transformation with courage and resolve comes from within—from knowing and believing in your authentic self.

Affirmation: I will seek to understand and be at peace with the paradoxes of change. I have the power to overcome all paradoxes.

Summary of Key Points:

- Adopt an attitude of acceptance and openness to change—shed your resistance and embrace the unknown.

- Listen to your heart and operate from what it tells you.

- Believe that only you hold the key to empowerment.

- Have the courage to be different—be you.

- Let go of old, familiar ways to meet the demand of doing more with less.

- Understand that paradoxes are a normal part of change.

- Respond rather than react to the paradoxes of change.

- Learn to be okay with questions.

- Find the right pace and speed for your work and personal lives.

- Strive for the blending of your work and personal lives, rather than balance.

Ask Yourself:

1. What are some of the paradoxes of change that I face in the workplace?

2. How does the organization deal with these paradoxes?

3. How do I personally deal with them?

4. Do I always present my authentic self? If not, what prevents me from doing so?

5. When I am my authentic self, what does it feel like?

6. Am I okay living with more questions than answers?

7. Am I afraid to embrace the unknown? Where do my fears come from?

8. What one new skill will I commit to learning each month?

Chapter 8
Seek Gainful Productivity in Your Calling

Never permit a dichotomy to rule your life, a dichotomy in which you hate what you do so you can have pleasure in your spare time. Look for a situation in which your work will give you as much happiness as your spare time.

Edward Bernays, 20th-Century American,
Founding Father of Public Relations

While many baby boomers followed their hearts back in the '60s and early '70s, most of us were "gainfully employed" in traditional jobs by the mid-'70s. We became much less preoccupied with following our passions and more focused on a good paycheck. When I told my family that I was leaving the corporate sector because I did not like it, they thought I was crazy. As a first generation college graduate in a professional capacity, their response was "Girl, you're crazy. Who cares if you like it or not, you are making good money." That counsel, I am sure, was echoed throughout households all across America, both white and black.

"Get a good paying job and be happy," they said. The common belief was that money would make you happy or, at least, it should.

Today, I am asking you to think about changing your frame of reference from the idea of gainful employment to one of "gainful productivity."

Being gainfully productive is different than being gainfully employed. "Gainful productivity" suggests that we create our own opportunities to earn a living doing something we love while at the same time adding value to society. Being gainfully productive means that, from time to time, we may not always be "employed" in the traditional sense during our "working" lives. We may be productively engaged in enhancing our skills by going back to school. We may take sabbaticals to renew our energy. We may find fulfillment in volunteer work. As we age, we may find that we need to take care of elderly parents. An associate of mine took six months off to take care of a terminally ill sister. Gainful productivity may have nothing to do with making money but everything to do with personal growth and development and being in service to others.

The mindshift from gainful employment to gainful productivity will also likely require a mindshift on how you manage your finances, which will be different from our "for the love of money," 20th-Century model. To shift, it is advisable to have at least one year's worth of income in savings. You may not "need" your entire current salary, but you should have some idea of how much is comfortable for you to live and support your family, if that is a reality for you. You should also understand what you are willing to sacrifice without regret.

Your ability to stay gainfully productive resides in your attitude about what it means to work and have a "job." The very definition of "job" is vastly different today from how we characterized it in the 20th century. What it means today to "get a good job and settle down" conjures up a totally different picture than what it meant during the industrial era.

The 20th-Century Definition of Job

The classic image of job meant that you entered into a "contract" with an employer to fulfill certain tasks at a given rate of pay. As we secured full-time employment either after high school or college, there was an implied expectation that if you performed adequately, the job was yours for as long as you wanted it, up to retirement age. We now refer to this attitude as "lifetime employment." We "settled" into a job that played a significant role in our lives and largely defined who we were as individuals. We set our standard of living based on that job and the assurance that it was secure.

Knowing someone's profession and, to some extent, where they worked allowed us to stereotype and make assumptions about that person—whether the job was something he or she liked, enjoyed, or even performed well. Many workers felt trapped or pigeonholed into certain roles, and were resigned to the attitude, "It's a job and pays good money. It allows me to support my family."

> *Whenever it is in any way possible, every boy and girl should choose as his life work some occupation, which he should like to do anyhow, even if he did not need the money.*
>
> Irish Blessing

The 21st-Century Definition of Job

In the 21st century, our jobs will definitely not be for a lifetime, will not define our whole being, and will not put us in confined boxes.

Rather than jobs, we will have "assignments" and "projects." As employers adopt concepts like "just-in-time" labor, we will increasingly be a society of contract workers without defined employment status and benefits.

The ranks of the self-employed are also growing exponentially. Some have grown weary of the chaotic business world; others were forced out, while still others are seizing the opportunity to take advantage of low entry costs to start a business afforded by technology. Author Daniel Pink, in his book *Free Agent Nation,* documents the trend of many workers becoming "free agents." He describes them as 30 million "job hopping, tech-savvy, fulfillment-seeking, self-employed, independent workers." Of these, about 13 million are operating micro-businesses. Pink estimates that these workers represent one-quarter to one-third of the workforce. In the "free agent nation," people serve their work ideals and personal needs rather than a specific company.[1]

Women and people of color are starting businesses at a rapid pace. According to a report prepared for the Minority Business Development Agency in September 2001, the growth rates in both number and gross receipts of minority-owned firms substantially exceeded those of non-minority businesses between 1992 and 1997.[2] There are also more women-owned businesses than ever before, growing at a rate faster than businesses overall, according to the U.S. Census Bureau's 1997 *Survey of Women-Owned Business Enterprises.*[3] This might suggest that the corporate world has failed to create adequately inclusive environments where everyone is able to reach his or her full potential. But because we have an infinite number of choices, when one door closes another will open, if we garner the faith to step out and not be confined in our thinking about what is possible.

The notion of unemployment is different in the 21st century. It will be common to have periods of time when you are between assignments. In the 20th century, we felt sorry for anybody who found himself or herself out of work. In the 21st century, people between assignments will be going for additional training, using the time for rejuvenation and revitalization, taking needed time to reassess their future, or giving service to the community. Due to the incredible pace of change, the assignments are likely to be so intense and all-consuming that it will be advantageous for us to have time-outs or sabbaticals.

These periods provide the opportunity to engage in other productive endeavors that enrich you personally and those around you. One of my friends is a contract technical writer on the West Coast. When she didn't have an assignment for three months, she enrolled in a magazine writing course at the University of California at Los Angeles. This was clearly a gainfully productive time. She used the opportunity to enhance her skill set by doing something for which she had a passion.

Virtual corporations where teams come together to perform specific tasks for a specific project and disband at the conclusion of the project will be a common way to work in the 21st century. These temporary organizations are cost-effective and allow the most appropriate talent for that one project to be deployed. My company has shifted to this approach. Rather than a full-time staff of 20, I now have a full-time administrative assistant, one part-timer and a cadre of consultants at my disposal with a variety of skills that I use, as needed, for various projects. I have assembled teams of interviewers to complete research projects as well as trainers to undertake large-scale educational endeavors.

I have created teams where marketing, human resources, project management, and product knowledge skills were required. This approach is more cost-effective for the client because it allows you to match the talent with the task.

Not only how you work, but where you work is likely to be different, too. Most of us think about going outside of the home to our place of employment, but the rise in home-based businesses is phenomenal. It is estimated that almost 30 million people operate home businesses and, according to the Michigan Small Business Development Center, a new home-based business starts every 11 seconds.[4]

Even if you work for a large company, chances are you will spend more time working away from the office — perhaps from home. Some will be assigned to client sites. Several Fortune 500 companies have given their sales teams laptops and require that they work from home. I have a friend who is a systems analyst. She goes into the office two days a week and works from her home the other three. I have a colleague who works for a large multinational company. He rises each morning, logs on to his computer, and spends the rest of the day at home engaged in communicating with his work colleagues in Europe.

When you work may also be different. My daughter will receive an electrical engineering degree this year. One of her job offers is with a federal agency. She can come into work anytime between 6 a.m. and 11 a.m.— the ultimate flex time schedule!

The redefinition of job as short-term, temporary assignments with breaks in between means that we must be self-motivated, creative, and self-sufficient. It is more important than ever before that we truly know our authentic selves, what we want from life, and what we are willing to do to achieve our dreams.

In the unstable world of work that awaits us, we must create our own opportunities for earning a living and being personally fulfilled. Our sense of well-being will not come from external sources (e.g., the boss, the affiliation with a particular organization, a specific job title), but rather from finding our center—our core, that which makes us who we are. As we come closer to finding our authentic selves, the fear of the unknown (e.g., Where will my next assignment come from?) dissipates. We are able to step out boldly and pursue our passions with great assurance that we manifest and attract all we need and desire.

Find Your Calling

As you think about work in the 21st century and strive to be gainfully productive, look for the opportunity to engage in your "ordained work." Your ordained work is that which you are "called" to do — work you feel passionate about and know you are competent at doing. You will find total fulfillment and happiness when you are able to be gainfully productive at what you love to do.

You may ask, "What about my bills?" There is great wisdom in the old adage: "Do what you love and the money will follow." But practically speaking, it is a journey. If you are not now engaged in what you think you are called to do — your passion—set a goal to discover what it is, and devise a plan to get you there.

Careers that are in vogue change over time. Where

the money was two years ago may not be where the "high paying" jobs are today. My daughter is an example. She is graduating with an electrical engineering and computer science degree from Georgia Institute of Technology (Georgia Tech) in May 2002. Due to many interrelated circumstances including the demise of the dot.com industry, the recent poor performance in the technology industry in general, and the impact of the September 11, 2001 terrorist attacks on America, young engineers are scrambling to find jobs.

Just two short years ago, there was a virtual shortage of engineers and computer scientists to the point where those who possessed the skills could name their price. There was to be a two-day job fair on Georgia Tech's campus this spring, which was reduced to just one day because so many companies canceled their scheduled appearances.

My point with this story is that if you go for the money and not your passion, you have to be willing to ride the rapidly changing tides. In my daughter's case, engineering and computers are what she likes. Her decision to pursue this field was based on both her interests and what seemed to be a "lucrative" and "stable" field. "Lucrative" and "stable" are moving targets but your passion is likely to be fairly "stable" for you over time. Therefore, seeking your life's work, in the end, has a higher probability of giving you all that you want — personal joy and economic prosperity.

> *The fact remains that the overwhelming majority of people who have become wealthy have become so thanks to work they found profoundly absorbing. The long-term study of people who eventually became wealthy clearly reveals that their "luck" arose from accidental dedication they had to an arena they enjoyed.*
>
> *Srully D. Blotnick, Contemporary American Author*

"Life work" is defined by cultural anthropologist Jennifer James as paid work, community work, personal/home maintenance and leisure activities. To the extent that your paid work intersects with one or more of your other life works, you are engaged in your passion, your ordained work (see Figure 6).

Figure 6

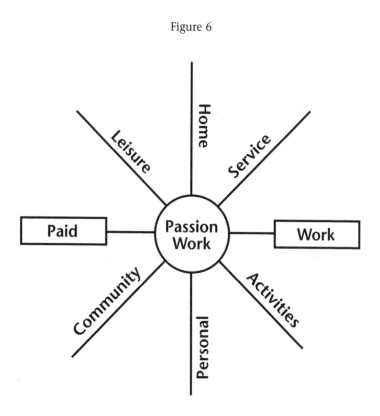

> **The biggest mistake people make in life is not trying to make a living doing what they most enjoy.**
>
> *Malcom Stevenson Forbes, Sr., 20th-Century*
> *American Publisher of* Forbes *Magazine*

Toward the end of my full-time employment in corporate America, I was miserable. I did not like what I was doing. I did not feel challenged. I knew that I had a lot more to offer, but I was stifled by corporate bureaucracy, and what I perceived to be narrow stereotypes of my ability. But what could I do? I felt trapped. I had to work. The company had sent me to an executive development program for my master's degree in business administration. Didn't I owe it some loyalty?

I was just about in tears every day from lack of challenge. The "straw that broke the camel's back" was when I learned that a major project I had been assigned to had been done by someone else a year earlier and resided in his desk drawer. I felt totally useless.

I evaluated my alternatives and I knew that I really wanted to do something very different. I decided to try starting my own company. When I left corporate America in 1984, it was not as common as it is today for people to have small consulting firms. As a matter of fact, it was so unusual that my local paper ran an article titled, "Woman Starts Business in Her Basement." I left with no guarantee of ever earning another cent.

It has been the greatest challenge of my life to run a business in these volatile times. Frequently, I did not know how I would meet payroll or pay the rent. But I have not given up. I have persevered. When I left my corporate job, one of the vice presidents said, "Let her go, she'll be back in six months begging for a job." I was determined not to let that happen. I had confidence that I could succeed at anything for which I really had a passion. If you want it badly enough, you will do what needs to be done to make it work. Les Brown, the motivational speaker, says, "You have to be hungry." I was hungry and I had a passion for what I was doing.

What I learned from my experience is that we do have choices. I did not have to stay in a job or at a company that did not meet my needs. Even though it may seem that there is no way out and that you must settle, please believe that you do not. It will not be easy. What I have found is that any endeavor that is truly worthwhile is not easy. There are no quick fixes in life. If you do not like your current job, set a goal for moving towards a profession for which you have a passion. Identify what you love to do and then envision yourself being gainfully productive in that field.

> *Adversity has the effect of eliciting talents, which in prosperous circumstances would have lain dormant.*
>
> Horace, Roman Poet (65 B.C.-8 B.C.), from the Epistles

I had an employee once who was miserable working for me as my administrative assistant. Even though she was a whiz at desktop publishing and had some wonderful skills that I could use, she was unfulfilled. She had a college degree in marketing, but had discovered that she really wanted to teach. That would require going back to school for additional credits to obtain her certification. She and her husband had just had their first child, and she couldn't see how she could manage it all. She came to work every day and put in a good effort, but we both knew that she was unhappy. It showed in the slowness of her gait and the deep sighs every time she was the least bit frustrated. She was merely going through the motions, and we both knew it.

I encouraged her to follow her dreams. I told her that if teaching was really her passion—if she wanted it badly enough—she would find a way to make it happen. Several months later, she left The Winters Group and took a marketing position at a credit union. About two years into that job, still unfulfilled, she enrolled in night school at a local college to complete the needed courses to teach.

I cannot tell you the difference today in this woman. The last time I saw her, she had completed her course requirements and was to begin student teaching soon. Her demeanor was totally different. There was a purpose in her walk and she smiled often. She said that even though her decision was a tremendous sacrifice with a toddler and that she had absolutely no time for herself, it was worth it and she would do it again.

> **Cut not the wings of your dreams for they are the heartbeat and the freedom of your soul.**
>
> *Flavia, Contemporary Inspirational Artist*

Another one of my friends personifies the baby boomer dilemma. She had been unfulfilled in her corporate job for some time and was yearning to spend more time with her children, but needed to provide for their future. She was unable to see her way out of her dilemma. She and her husband, in their late '40s, knew no other way to maintain their livelihood. She kept telling me she felt trapped and wanted to spend more time with her two young boys.

Having been through a similar experience 15 years before, I assured her that there is life after working in corporate America. She struggled mightily with her decision for over two years and was miserable during the transition.

Finally, when the company transferred her position out of state, she was forced to make a decision. She decided to pursue a new career as a financial advisor — one that could potentially be more lucrative than her current job, but would also afford her the flexibility that she and her family needed. Today, she is like a new woman.

Another example is a special friend of mine who ran a security business for 16 years before deciding to follow his passion of writing and publishing. The weight that has been lifted from him is evident in his physical appearance and health. He looks younger, feels better physically, and is joyful.

Also, one of my college classmates became a pediatrician, but she had a passion for baking. Some years ago, she decided to do both. She is a part-time doctor and also runs a small bakery.

> *You will recognize your own path when you come upon it, because you will suddenly have all the energy and imagination you will ever need.*
>
> Jerry Gillies, Contemporary American Author

I share these stories with you to give you the courage that you might need to get out of a dead-end job and into something that really makes you happy — something that would make you jump out of bed in the morning with great anticipation.

I am not suggesting that you go out and immediately resign from a job that you dislike. The reality is that sometimes we are forced, in order to make a living, to do work that is unfulfilling. What I am suggesting, though, is that you don't settle for such a job indefinitely. You have choices. The choices are yours. It may require sacrifice and retraining, but the choice is to be miserable, or energized and happy.

To survive in the 21st century of rapidly advancing technology and constant change, you must love what you do and, conversely, do only what you love. This helps you to manage change more effectively. We are spending more and more time engaged in our "work." Economists estimate that we are working an average of one-third more than we did 30 years ago.

I don't want to suggest that it is easy because it isn't. Decisions about how you will ultimately earn a living are some of the most difficult life decisions that you have to make. Baby boomers were lured into thinking the decisions were about the money. I am suggesting that the decisions should have nothing to do with the money, but with what you feel called to do.

> *When our eyes see our hands doing the work of our hearts, the circle of creation is completed inside us, the doors of our souls fly open and love steps forth to heal everything in sight.*
>
> Michael Bridge, *Contemporary Professor of Commercial Law at the University of Nottingham, England*

Employers in the 21st century need people who want to do

what they are doing. Needless to say, you will be more productive if you really enjoy what you do. It has been my observation—based on more than 9,000 interviews conducted by The Winters Group at Fortune 500 corporations, associations and government agencies—that entry-level to highly-skilled workers consistently deliver the same message: They cannot do their best work because of the chaotic environment created by ongoing downsizings, mergers, and acquisitions.

Chances are then, as you are reading this, you are thinking, "I do not do what I like at work, and I am not doing what I do best. I am doing what I have been told to do. After all, I need a job and I must earn a living." Or, maybe you were doing what you loved and were a victim of downsizing and felt forced to take a job that puts food on the table and pays the bills. Perhaps your interests have changed over the years. Maybe you did love what you were doing, but for whatever reason, do not find it fulfilling anymore. Or maybe you are in a career that will become obsolete because of advances in technology, and you are forced to think of what else you like to do.

> *Get happiness out of your work or you may never know what happiness is.*
>
> Elbert Hubbard, 20th-Century American Author

Everybody has a "calling" in life. Each one of us has a unique gift to offer the world. We sometimes spend a lifetime trying to figure out what it is. We are sometimes afraid to get in touch with our true feelings and passions, or we may have convinced ourselves that we are helpless victims of circumstance with no way out. If you have courage, there is always an alternative. Life is too short to spend so much of your time in a job that is unfulfilling. Find your "calling." Find a way to make a living doing what excites and stimulates you. Never settle. You owe it to the world to share your gift with us.

As we embark upon the new world of work in the 21st century, you can ill afford to just collect a paycheck. Figure out where your passion intersects with your competencies, and go for it. It may mean that you must totally retrain, but think of the long-term benefits of doing something that you like and that adds value to your family and society at the same time.

Embrace a goal — a new way of working that you believe would really be your passion. Next, establish a realistic time frame, and make a list of what you need to do to reach the goal (e.g., pay off bills, enroll in school, gain family support, etc.).

> *You must have long-term goals to keep from being frustrated with the short-term failures.*
>
> *Charles C. Noble, Retired President and CEO, C.T. Main Corp.*

Consult with experts in the area that you have chosen. Take one day at a time, and when you think that you want to give up, pick up this book and read this section again. Hang in there. Extend the time frame if necessary, but never, ever give up. We often underestimate the amount of time required to reach a goal and become frustrated and give up. Nothing that is worthwhile is quick, easy, or without pain.

Affirmation: I will strive to be gainfully productive, shedding old notions of "job" and expanding my possibilities to lead a rewarding life. I will find my "calling."

Summary of Key Points:

- The definition of "job" has changed.

- What you do, where, when and how you do it will be different.

- Independent contractors or "free agents" will dominate the labor pool.

- Seek gainful productivity rather than gainful employment.

- Your income flow is likely to fluctuate in the future.

- Your attitude about managing your finances will have to change.

- Your passion work is the intersection of what you love to do and what you are paid to do.

- When you are engaged in your calling, you offer your best self to the world.

Ask Yourself:

1. Do I know the difference between gainful employment and "gainful productivity"?

2. Do I have a narrow, traditional view of "job"?

3. Do I feel trapped in an unfulfilling career?

4. How can I become gainfully productive doing what I love?

5. What financial adjustments would I need to make to become totally gainfully productive?

6. What would I be doing if I were gainfully productive?

7. What is my passion? Do I know what my "calling" is?

8. What would it feel like to be engaged in my "ordained work"?

9. What is my plan of action to pursue my "calling"?

Chapter 9
Turn Wishful Thinking into Breakthrough Thinking

One does not discover new lands without consenting to lose sight of the shore for a very long time.

André Gide

In the preceding chapters, I discussed a variety of important personal transformations. For any of these to happen, you will need to stretch yourself toward a new way of thinking and to develop a willingness to break through barriers and boundaries. Whether you continue in a corporate environment, find new ways to work productively in your present field, or go out and start your own business, you will need to tackle each barrier and overcome it.

Boundaries Set At Birth

Social scientists estimate that most of us use only 10 percent of our potential. What keeps us from self-actualizing? There are lots of barriers, but the main one for baby boomers is that we have been conditioned from childhood to be cautious, not to take too many risks, and to be safe. Parents begin protecting and putting limits on their children in infancy. Our good intentions often squelch exploration that could lead to creativity and innovation.

The boundaries that we set up are sometimes very narrow and, of course, influence us for the rest of our lives. My mother was overly protective of me. She only wanted what was in my best interest, and she set up parameters based on her assumptions about what was for my good. For example, I have a natural tendency towards my left hand. She forced me to use my right hand. To this day, I have more strength on my left side and use my left hand to brush my hair. My parents had a list of *don't*s and *can't*s that was much, much longer than the list of *why don't you try.* I wasn't encouraged to go into sports because I might be hurt. There were certain children whom I wasn't allowed to play with, and books and television programs that I wasn't allowed to read or see. My parents tried to "protect" me, but in so doing, they also limited my natural curiosity and ability to self-discover.

While I maintained that I would never put such limits on my children, I am afraid that as I look back, I tended to set boundaries which I see now were limiting. My son, Joe, has always been big. At the day care center, he towered over other children. The staff at the center said that he often unintentionally hurt other children. In our quest to avoid such occurrences, we taught him to be passive and it later showed up when he played basketball in high school. He had great technical skills, but he was totally non-aggressive. He had been so conditioned as a small child to back away for fear of hurting someone that he could not change his mindset on the court.

To a greater or lesser degree, we were all taught the "boundaries" early on in life; many of us have not extended our limits or, as adults, have developed "fears." For example, I never learned to swim. Even though I took swimming in school, I did not want to get my hair wet, so I didn't want to go in the deep end of the pool. To this day, I am afraid of water and will not venture into water that is above my head.

It is in these uncharted territories—the breaking of boundaries—and conquering the fears of the unknown that breakthrough thinking and inner power exists. Our unleashed potential is in the deep end of the pool.

A smooth sea never made a skilled mariner.

English Proverb

Breakthrough Thinkers are Needed for 21st-Century Challenges

No matter what your employment situation, your boss or your clients will require that you be able to think critically, problem-solve, and use common sense. The old adage of "check your brain at the door" is passé. No longer will jobs be routine, with employees repeating the same steps over and over again.

Automation has replaced the need for "hands" to assemble products, but constant and rapid change necessitate that employees be able to think of new and better ways to accomplish the goals of the organization. If you work for a nonprofit, there is the ever-increasing risk of de-funding. If you work for a retail establishment, changing demographics make it difficult to keep updated with what the customer wants. If you work for a high technology firm, new competitive companies arrive on the scene daily with better and less expensive products. If you are self-employed, you must constantly find new contracts. In the New Economy, the full court press is on. Every team member is essential.

Every brain is needed just to keep pace and hopefully stay one step ahead.

> *Like water flowing from an underground spring, human creativity is the well-spring greening the desert of toil and effort, and much of what stifles us in the workplace is the immense unconscious effort on the part of organizations and individuals alike to dam the flow.*
>
> David Whyte

The U.S. Department of Labor, through its Secretary's Commission on Achieving Necessary Skills (SCANS), outlined a list of 17 foundation skills that every worker will need to succeed in the 21st century. They are divided into four categories: basic skills, thinking skills, people skills, and personal qualities. There is an interesting new emphasis on *thinking.*[1]

Basic Skills: Reading, writing, speaking, listening, and knowing arithmetic and mathematical concepts

Thinking Skills: Reasoning, making decisions, thinking creatively, solving problems, seeing things in the mind's eye, and knowing how to learn

People Skills: Ability to work in a team, respect for diversity, interpersonal skills, civility

Personal Qualities: Responsibility, self-esteem, sociability, self-management, integrity, and honesty

In addition, the Commission outlined competencies that you will need to actually perform the jobs in the 21st century.

Workplace Skills:

Resources — Identifying, organizing, planning, and allocating time, money, materials, and workers

Interpersonal Skills — Negotiating, exercising leadership, respecting diversity, teaching others new skills, serving clients and customers, and participating as a team member

Information Skills—Using computers to process information and acquiring, evaluating, organizing, maintaining, interpreting, and communicating information

Systems Skills—Understanding systems, monitoring and correcting system performance, and improving and designing systems

Technology Utilization Skills—Selecting technology, applying technology to a task, and maintaining and troubleshooting technology

It is clear that the capacity to think, innovate, and create new and better ways will be a necessity in any work environment. Breakthrough thinkers will be in large demand.

> *The intellectual equipment needed for the job of the future is the ability to define problems, quickly assimilate relevant data, conceptualize and reorganize the information, make deductive and inductive leaps with it, ask hard questions about it, discuss findings with colleagues, work collaboratively to find solutions, and then convince others.*
>
> Robert Reich

I think and think for months and years; 99 times the conclusion is false. The 100th time I am right.

Albert Einstein

What is a Breakthrough Thinker?

Breakthrough thinking first means that you believe that all things are possible. There are no *"can'ts," "never's,"* or *"impossible's"* in a breakthrough thinker's vocabulary. As a breakthrough thinker, you are always questioning how to do it better, faster, and smarter. You believe in "good, better, best. Never let it rest until your good gets better and your better gets best." Breakthrough thinkers believe in their own capacity to achieve abundantly more tomorrow than they do today. They believe in limitless possibilities, infinite choices, and no boundaries.

I could use 100 people who do not know there is such a word as impossible.

Henry Ford, 20th-Century American
Industrialist and Pioneer Automobile Manufacturer

Breakthrough thinkers constantly challenge the status quo. They question "why" or "why not." Breakthrough thinkers are tenacious and do not give up even though their ideas may be shot down hundreds of times. I was told by a well-meaning guidance counselor that a four-year degree was too lofty a goal for someone like me. Not only did I say, "I'll show you," but I was on the dean's list most semesters and became the youngest and the first African-American female trustee of the University of Rochester. I was told that I could not have an assignment in human resources during my first year in corporate America because I was too young and inexperienced. Within three months, I landed an assignment in human resources. We can all break through barriers. It is not wishful thinking. It is *breakthrough* thinking that makes the difference.

No doubt we can name famous people from the beginning of time who were breakthrough thinkers. But the capacity to make quantum leaps in the workplace resides in every individual. What about the Minnesota Mining & Manufacturing Company (3M) workers who discovered Post-it® Notes? The engineering team was trying to make a very strong glue and while that was a failure, someone decided to put the formula to use as what we now know as Post-it® Notes.

Breakthrough thinking is much more likely to occur if you have a passion for what you do. You are more likely to be motivated to be inventive and creative when you are engaged in your passion work.

Everyone is capable of breakthrough thinking. It requires the courage to take risks even though the consequences might be negative. It requires a strong belief in yourself and that you have something unique to offer. It requires the willingness to let go and invoke spirit.

Far better it is to dare mighty things, even though checkered by failure, than to take rank with those who neither enjoy much or suffer much, because they live in the gray twilight that knows not victory nor defeat.

Theodore Roosevelt, 26th President of the United States

So many of us become stuck in the routine of our jobs—after awhile we just accept the process. We sometimes get stuck because we are so busy juggling the many demands of the job that there is no time for quality thinking about why and how we perform our work. Breakthrough thinking is more likely to occur when time is set aside to question processes and procedures. But such time may not be allocated in an official way. It is up to you to set aside time on a regular basis to challenge and reexamine why you do what you do in the way that you do it. This constant questioning and reexamination will definitely lead to new and enhanced methods. Breakthrough thinking happens when you are willing to let go of assurances, guarantees, and routines.

> **When we are not sure, we are alive.**
>
> *Graham Greene, 20th-Century British Author*

Increasing Your Capacity for Breakthrough Thinking

There are an infinite number of techniques for releasing

your power for breakthrough thinking, from literally "taking a walk" to more structured exercises to opening up to the deep, dark places of the soul, which we discussed in Chapter 3.

We can learn from Eastern philosophies such as Buddhism and Taoism. They believe that we cannot create from the control and illusion of our minds. We must go beyond the mind and its power, and just let the mind go free to express anything. Letting the mind go will undoubtedly take us to our spirit. As soon as we "try to create," we are in a controlling mode. We have to learn to "lose control," so to speak, and let the mind "be." Instead of forcing anything, let it come. It is not productive to strive for "originality" because it springs from the exact opposite of striving. Simply let it flow.

When I am writing, if I just keep the words coming from my fingertips as I enter the text into the computer without really thinking about how I am saying it — sort of a stream of consciousness — I am always amazed at what cogent, creative text I create. When I am consciously concerned about the flow, it doesn't seem to come forth.

> **Don't think. Thinking is the enemy of creativity. It's the self-conscious. Anything self-conscious is lousy. You can't try to do things. You simply must do things.**
>
> Ray Bradbury, *Contemporary American Science-Fiction Writer*

Activating the creative genius in you happens by letting go — emptying your head of preconceived notions, assumptions, premises, rules, conventions, traditions, and ideas.

In the industrial era of assembly lines, standard operating procedures, and the routine, creativity was not expected or required. As baby boomers who have been indoctrinated with processes that foster conformity and little change, unleashing our creative powers is hard for many of us to do. We were brought up in a work world of absolutes: *yeses* or *nos, this or that, either, or, only one truth, only one answer.*

The reality of today is that there are few absolutes: many

maybes, lots of *boths, ands,* zillions of it *depends,* and an infinite number of questions.

Taking time to just be — to become an empty vessel and allow random thoughts to enter your psyche — is probably not something that is encouraged if you are employed in a traditional company. If the boss were to stop by and ask, "What are you doing?" and you responded, "Being an empty vessel to ignite my creativity," well, you may be out seeking your passion work before you are ready!

So how, when, and where you choose to engage your power for breakthrough thinking is always a consideration.

In a strategic planning workshop that I facilitated a couple of years ago, the group was charged with turning around a failing business. The brainstorming elicited traditional solutions. This was a technical group of fairly conservative people. Unplanned, I got up and started to dance around the room chanting, "Follow the leader...leader...leader. Follow the leader." Slowly everyone joined in and we had a "conga" line around the room with everyone following my gestures. Wow! Talk about taking folks out of their comfort zone! I took a risk (of being fired as a consultant) but in the end (though it took a while), it loosened people up and they were able to begin to think differently. My motto is: Whatever it takes, do it!

Here are some ideas for stimulating your ability for break-through thinking.

Issue: You have been downsized. You need breakthrough thinking to help you plan a course of action. You want to move towards your passion work.

1. Connect the seemingly unconnected.

Seeing the interconnectedness of everything in the universe will augment your ability to release your creative powers. We tend to segment our lives—work, home, religion, etc. By thinking holistically, we are able to apply "learnings" from other areas of our lives to our work.

Newton's Laws were inspired by what on the surface were unconnected events. Based on his account (contradicting the popular story of his being hit by a falling apple), the concept of universal gravitation was conceived when he saw an apple falling, and, at the same time, he noticed the moon in the sky. Seeing these images simultaneously gave him the thought, "What if the same laws controlled the falling apple and the moon orbiting the earth?" This led him to develop the laws of mechanics.

Ask yourself questions about things that may not seem connected. For example, ask: What does my ability to earn a living have to do with the expression of my faith? How is my age connected to where I shop? (You may find none, but stretch yourself!)

Make lists of random words that just come into your head. Find a connection to them.

Example:
Write...air...sad...personal...calm...determined...
understand...angry...prepared.
This is a list of words that came to my mind given the problem of being downsized and looking for my passion work.

241

The connections I see are: "I have strong emotions (sadness and anger) which could thwart my need to move forward, but I am also determined and calm. I should write about my feelings."

Pick random objects from around your house or office. Is there a connection? If so, what is it?

Read the dictionary. My son taught me this one. I saw him pouring over a dictionary one day. When I asked him what he was doing, he said, "Reading the dictionary." I thought it was a bit strange but he said that it not only helped him to improve his vocabulary, but also helped him to think new thoughts and make new connections.

2. Change your normal habits and observe what is around you in nature.

Something as simple as taking a different route to the grocery store can release breakthrough thoughts if you are observant and use your imagination. What do you see taking this route that you have not seen before? How can you relate it to the issue of finding your passion work? What does a solitary tree—barren in the middle of winter—tell you about your situation? Maybe the lesson is this: For everything there is a season, and this is your season of rest and renewal.

3. Make a list of questions.

I keep six honest serving men. They taught me all I knew: Their names are What and Why and When and How and Where and Who.

Rudyard Kipling, 20th-Century British Author,
from Just So Stories

Why am I out of a job?

Why did I work here?

Why do I feel like I do?

What did I enjoy about this work?

What didn't I enjoy?

When do I feel most energized?

Where am I most at peace?

Who is important to me?

How do I work best?

4. Turn wishful thinking into breakthrough thinking.

We all dream about a perfect state — what we wish for, but think is out of our realm of possibilities. Continue to engage in wishful thinking by making a "wish list." I wish I could do (_____) every day. I wish I never had to do (_____) again.

Now ask yourself what would have to happen for your wishes to become realities. Don't say, "Well, that could never happen. There is too big a barrier." In other words, do not evaluate the viability of the change that would have to occur, simply list it. Now prioritize your wish list by the things you most want to happen. It may be the least likely in your mind based on "what would have to happen to make it a reality." If it is what you most want, regardless of the perceived barriers, it is absolutely the one to go after! Look "unrealistically" at the barriers. What are the ways you can overcome them? Notice I said look "unrealistically." We have been taught to think in a "realistic" way. Realism is a moving target today. It wasn't realistic 15 years ago to think that we could communicate with the world by e-mail, instantaneously by the mere push of a button. Is it easy to think "unrealistically"? Is it easy to eliminate barriers? Of course not! The goal would not be worth it if it were!

5. Surface and test your assumptions.

What are the assumptions that you have about your life, work, and circumstances? What if these assumptions were not true? What are some new assumptions that you can generate for yourself?

For example, you might assume that your next job will be in the same industry as the one from which you were downsized. What if you just reversed that assumption: Your next job will not be in the same industry.

See what new thinking that can bring!

6. Always look for multiple solutions/multiple sources.

As I said earlier, we were trained to think in absolutes and usually do not exhaust all of our potential options. "Yep, this one sounds good! Let's go with it!" It is more expedient to get to a solution and then to action, but don't jump too quickly. Continually ask, "but what if," or "what about," or "what else." As we say when brainstorming, no idea is too outlandish.

7. Draw it!

Visual stimulation can be a powerful idea generator. I am a "doodler." I am certainly by no stretch of the imagination an artist, but I draw shapes and images in a random manner to see what notions they conjure up. I also study art that I am exposed to, not only for meaning, but to spur new ideas.

8. Build a community of conversation partners.

Connecting with groups of like- and unlike-minded individuals can foster breakthrough thinking.

As an entrepreneur running a small business, it is easy to become isolated with only a few peers to share experiences and explore new ideas. To expand that circle, I have sought groups where, for example, each participant was given the opportunity to present an issue. The group would then help to bring out new ways to think about the problem.

Sometimes, we are just too close to our own issues to see the myriad possibilities. When I had about 10 employees, I was wrestling with the challenge of maintaining the level of business required to sustain that amount of overhead (fixed costs). One of the members of the think tank said, "It seems like you are working for your employees rather than them working for you." I had never thought of it that way before. It was from this exchange that I conceived the notion of restructuring as a virtual corporation, bringing the required talent together for projects as needed.

> *We become what we think about.*
>
> *Earl Nightingale*

This was a true breakthrough for The Winters Group. With the large number of highly talented people being displaced from corporate America starting one-person consulting operations, I had ready access to a cadre of specialists. I may have come to this breakthrough on my own, but having others provide a new frame of reference for me to think about my issue propelled me to a clearer understanding of what the problem really was and how I could solve it.

While all of these idea-generating techniques can be useful (and there are hundreds more, from simple brainstorming to mind-mapping), the prerequisite for breakthrough thinking is for you to be open to dream the impossible, to think the unthinkable, and to imagine the unimaginable, the good, the bad, the positive, the negative, the *can't*s, the *should*s, the *shouldn't*s, the *must's*, and the *mustn't*s. Immerse yourself as deeply as possible into the unknown, the uncomfortable, the unexplained — not just one time but as often as you can release yourself to your soul.

Offer Your Brilliance to the World

Breakthrough thinking is not the sole dominion of management. Everybody in an organization should feel a deep sense of responsibility for thinking about new possibilities.

In the employee research that The Winters Group conducts, I all too often hear, "I'm not paid enough for that" or "They will just shoot down my ideas anyway." In the 21st-Century work world, equating your status or rate of pay with the amount of innovative thinking that you will do is surely career suicide. I recently read a chat room remark from a disgruntled, downsized employee who said that his employer had gained the benefits of all of his creative ideas. He felt that the employer had, in essence, stolen his work without adequate remuneration. I suggest that the motivation for engaging in breakthrough thinking is not about the potential reward from your employer, but the intrinsic payback that only you can enjoy. If it is your idea, you can build on it and make it better for the next assignment.

For many of us today, our ideas are our products and vice versa. We become very protective of our creative thoughts. Intellectual property right law has become a very lucrative practice as inventors, consultants, writers, and others try to avoid misuse, plagiarism, and outright theft of their ideas. While these are real concerns, try not to let undue fear stifle your brilliance.

Nobody can think it exactly the way you do. Nobody can say it exactly the way you would. Nobody can deploy it just like you would because you are one of a kind. As long as you do not fall prey to conforming or copying and comparing to what another has done, it will always be yours. You may have to "fight" for it. (That is why there are intellectual property right laws and lawyers.) Again, I did not say it would be easy, but no one can take the essence of your being—those private places where only you can venture, where your most creative self exists.

Affirmation: I will turn wishful thinking into breakthrough thinking, not because I expect more money or position from my employer, but because I am personally challenged and motivated by thinking the impossible and coming up with revolutionary new ideas to significantly improve my work and life. I am committed to allocating time each day just for thinking. I believe in my infinite power.

Summary of Key Points:

- We do not engage in breakthrough thinking because we are taught from an early age to be cautious, to play it safe.

- We must unlearn the behaviors and attitudes that prevent us from unleashing our limitless potential.

- Breakthrough thinking is about a state of being that allows you to completely open your soul.

- Breakthrough thinking happens when we challenge every belief and assumption that we hold.

- Allocate time every day to allow yourself to dream, to just be open and receptive.

- Engage in specific exercises that will enhance creative thinking.

- Redefine rejection. Do not view it as a defeat, but as a challenge to keep at it. Not all of your ideas will be adopted immediately, and some will never be adopted.

Ask Yourself:

1. What are my own self-imposed limits? What boxes have I put around myself?

2. Do I believe in my limitless power?

3. What small risk am I willing to take to begin to expand the possibilities?

4. Why do I think this way about (_____)? What evidence do I have that this is true? What if I changed my assumptions? What are some new assumptions that would allow me to eliminate some of my barriers?

5. Do I limit my breakthrough abilities with fear? What am I afraid of?

6. Where/When/How do I do my best breakthrough thinking?

Chapter 10

Bustin' Loose

Keep what you got until you get what you need, ya' all.

Got to give a lot just to get what you need,

sometimes, ya' all.

I feel like bustin' loose...

bustin' loose in the evening...

bustin' loose can be pleasin'...

bustin' loose makes you feel fine...

talkin' about Bustin' Loose...

Lyrics from Song Written and Performed by
Chuck Brown and the Soul Searchers

If you have made it this far in the book, you are likely having one of several emotions right now. You are positively motivated to embrace change and find your passion work. You are still skeptical. Or you absolutely think my advice is out in left field.

You may "buy" my theories about baby boomers and how our values have shaped our thinking about work. Most would probably admit that self-awareness is necessary to navigate successfully in an ever-changing world and that you can do more to assure that you understand self. Hopefully, seeing the paradoxes of change and examining your natural response to change, will help you to deal a little bit better with the chaos in the work world. I tried to offer a different way of framing your attitudes about work by inviting you to seek gainful productivity in your calling as contrasted to gainful employment. I postulated that none of these shifts are possible without breaking through personal barriers to change.

But let's face it. It "ain't" easy. We are baby boomers, set in our ways, with deep-seated habits, traditions, and beliefs. After all, as the saying goes, "You can't teach an old dog new tricks."

For some of us, the kind of radical change that I am talking about seems out of reach. You have gotten this far in life, and you feel like you have little energy to totally transform. After all, the older we get, the harder it is to learn and change.

That all may very well be true. But if you are 50 years old, you probably have at least 10 more years to work, if not 20. The economy may dictate that you work longer. Social Security is not guaranteed. We are healthier and more vital for more years today. Millions of baby boomers are starting second careers—many of them following their passions. You, too, can find your passion. It is not too late.

But it is still hard. You may be somewhat complacent believing that if the downsizing would only stop, you would be fine. Or if your organization doesn't go through any more mergers, you should be set for at least the next five years.

It is the *if* part that gets us every time. Things happen that have a devastating impact on us over which we have no control.

For thousands of people personally impacted by September 11, 2001, change was not a choice. Their lives were permanently and irrevocably transformed through no fault of their own. It is hard and will continue to be hard to deal with the tragedy for many years to come.

It is human nature to want life to be predictable, secure, and stable. There is nothing wrong with desiring to know that you will have a paycheck next week or next year. We make important decisions based on assumptions about the level of stability (lack of change) in our lives. We don't like it when our lives are disrupted by situations that cause abrupt change.

> *We must accept finite disappointment, but we must never lose infinite hope.*
>
> *Martin Luther King, Jr.*

Adopt an "I'm Ready" Mindset

Deep down inside we know that change is inevitable. Little changes occur constantly in our lives. We move, we change jobs, we change our diets, we make a new friend, or we lose an old friend. Some changes we like, others we don't. I maintain that in today's volatile world there will be more big changes than ever before. We need to be prepared. We need to learn to understand the dynamics of change and how it personally impacts us. Understanding yourself, how you naturally respond to change, and what your personal barriers are, will help you to manage in the tough times. Taking personal responsibility for your own functioning and resisting the urge to blame others or become the helpless victim will keep you centered when chaos surrounds you.

Business authors Michael Beer and Nitin Nohria say that people change to the extent that the level of dissatisfaction, the compelling vision of the future, and the first step to establish momentum is greater than the resistance, as shown in the equation below.[1]

DVF>R
D = Dissatisfaction
V = Compelling Vision of the Future
F = First Steps to Establish Momentum
R = Resistance (e.g., what you think you are giving up—fear)

We all resist change to some degree. It has to do with our survival instincts, comfort with the familiar, and fear of the unknown.

Sometimes it takes a significant emotional event, such as the sudden loss of a job or a tragedy like September 11, 2001, to create enough momentum and dissatisfaction for change. When change is sudden, abrupt, unexpected, and life-altering, it can be devastating enough to paralyze us.

I suggest you adopt an "I'm ready" mindset, which fosters the belief that there are no guarantees — my situation could radically change tomorrow and I am prepared to deal with whatever may present itself. The extent to which we understand that there will be fear and resistance and a new vision may have to be developed, will make our ability to move to the next level much easier.

Having an "I'm ready" mindset means that you always have a plan *B* and *C* and maybe even *D*. I am amazed by the number of people who call me when they find themselves unemployed and admit that they had not thought about what they would do if this happened. They do not have an updated résumé, they have not kept their skills current, and they have not even conceived that they could pursue their passions. They are like the wet babies who expect that someone is going to come and change them so that they are dry and feel better. We may be baby boomers but we are not babies — nobody is going to change us but us, and nobody can assure our future but us.

> *If things don't turn out as we wish, we should wish for them as they turn out.*
>
> Aristotle, Greek Philosopher, 384 B.C. – 322 B.C.

The Stages of Change

There are essentially three stages in the change process: (1) the identification of the need or desire; (2) transition (chaos); and (3) the new state, which I call "bustin' loose." There is a little story about "bustin' loose." I was asked by a client to give a presentation on change to about 400 leaders in the organization. It was a traditional company having significant difficulty moving from an industrial-era to a knowledge-era mindset. Intellectually everyone knew there was a need for change — big change. They had embarked on a multiyear culture change journey and were in the middle of the transition or chaos stage. And they were experiencing a lot of pain.

I sat down at my computer one morning to begin to draft the presentation. I wanted to inspire and motivate while, at the same time, give them some straight talk. I closed my eyes, put my fingers on the keyboard and let my mind go. The first thing that appeared was the song, "Bustin' Loose." (A little breakthrough thinking, huh?) I remembered how much I liked that rhythm and blues tune of the '80s. It was a great dance song, which I used to "bust loose" to on the dance floor. Dancing to this song made me feel free, unbridled, changed. That was it! In order for the company to move from chaos to the desired state, my client needed to be willing to "bust loose."

The organization was stuck. It had gotten through phase one of identifying the need and the development of the strategy. It was now trying to implement the change, and it was so hard. Individuals, while well-meaning, just didn't know how to "be" any other way. They wanted a formula, a quick fix. Sorry, it "ain't" easy. I believe changing a culture happens one person at a time, which is why I focus on personal transformation. Everybody has to "bust loose" in his or her own way.

Let's look at the three stages from a personal perspective. In stage one, the need or desire can be triggered by something internal or external. Maybe you are bored with your current work or life situation, or there is a chronic problem in your life that just won't go away, or maybe the need is borne out of an external event, such as a loss of job. We often try to ignore the need for change. Our defense and survival mechanisms kick in, and we rationalize why it won't work.

But once we commit to the change, there may be a feeling of excitement and exhilaration. You have a focus now. You have made the decision. You begin to outline the steps you need to take. (e.g., You decide to enroll in a night course to gain new skills. You make the necessary phone calls and go on-line for the course descriptions, etc.). It's kind of fun. You are making progress. It is best to start small, with little steps towards the new state. If you try to take too large a leap from where you are, failure to achieve may move you swiftly back into a rut. As Chapter 8 pointed out, we have lots of self-imposed boundaries. To reach breakthrough thinking, you should initially make a slow move into uncharted territory. Plan to quickly become comfortable, however, with the little changes so that you can leap to the bigger ones in short order.

> *He had the deed half done, who has made a beginning.*
>
> Horace

The next stage is transition (chaos). There is a great deal of frustration and tension in this stage. There are many paradoxes to face, as addressed in Chapter 7. Even if you have outlined the steps to the new desired state, there is a strong pull to revert to the comfort level of the old and familiar. In the transition phase, old paradigms collapse and your sense of self begins to change. You typically feel vulnerable and maybe even powerless to act.

You may find yourself exhibiting the behaviors described in one of the six responses to change outlined in Chapter 6. Maybe you are faking it to yourself and others, which will surely catch up to you sooner or later. Maybe you are in a fearful mode, behaving in a self-protectionist, paranoid way. You have enrolled in a course but you find the material very difficult. The class is on a night that conflicts with a commitment that your spouse has, and there is no one to attend to the children. You are feeling tired all of the time because you have to take the extra time to study. When someone asks how it is going, you don't want to admit that it is hard, so you fake it and say, "Great!"

It is in the chaotic transitional phase of change that it is critical for us to know ourselves and be able to manage our own functioning. Ask yourself constantly, "What is going on with me right now? Why am I feeling this way?"

To successfully move from transition to the new state of "bustin' loose," we must learn to:

- Live with the paradoxes of change
- Listen to ourselves—listen to our emotions, our "guts"
- Be okay with having more questions than answers
- Be patient with ourselves and others
- Routinely examine our actions as to whether they are congruent with our values
- Take responsibility for managing our own functioning—constantly examining where we are at any given time
- Be okay with feeling "at risk"
- Engage in breakthrough thinking

None of what I am suggesting is easy. Major change that transforms you will likely be very painful. There is no way to avoid the pain. You cannot go around it, over it, or under it. You have to go through it. But you can manage the pain.

You can choose your response to the pain to ease it and to make the transition bearable.

The choice is the type of mindset that you adopt while going through change. The ability to remain optimistic, hopeful, and passionate rests in your hands. No one can take away your optimism and positive outlook.

> *You gain strength, courage and confidence by every experience in which you really stop to look fear in the face. You are able to say to yourself, 'I have lived through this horror. I can take the next thing that comes along.' You must do the thing you think you cannot do.*
>
> Eleanor Roosevelt

The third phase, the "bustin' loose" new state, is only possible when you are free—when the new place invites you to step forward with wild abandon. You are dancing to the lyrics of "Bustin' Loose"—shaking and gyrating with excitement and passion—mind, body, and spirit in one accord. When you can see it, taste it, hear it, and smell it, you want it and feel it in the depths of your soul. Then, and only then, can it become a possibility. You are transformed — born anew. The old way holds no appeal. Much of what it was is forgotten. You stayed in the class and even though you failed the first test, one day, it all clicked. You understand the material. It is mid-semester — not too late to still get a decent grade. You love the material. You are learning a great deal. It is exciting. The scheduling conflict still exists, but it doesn't seem nearly as devastating as it did a month ago. Your friend has agreed to help transport the children.

When I decided to leave corporate America and start my own business, it was one of the greatest turning points in my life, as I mentioned in Chapter 3. I was extremely fearful of leaving a "secure" situation for one that was totally unfamiliar to me. I engaged in breakthrough thinking with myself and others. I brainstormed, made a list of pros and cons, and sought advice from others already in business, but still I had a constant knot in my stomach — so much uncertainty. What if it did not work? What if I incurred large debt? There were so many questions and so few answers. I had to call on all of my skills for coping with fear, as outlined in Chapter 6.

And then one day, I "busted loose" from the chaos phase. There was no particular fanfare, no specific significant emotion to which I can point. But suddenly, there was the vision. I could see it and feel it, and I knew there was no turning back. I sat with myself for hours reveling in the picture of my new being. I could describe what The Winters Group was going to be. I wrote a vision and a mission. I saw myself working with clients and developing strategies. I could see what the office would look like and the type of people I would employ. The time had come. It could not have been sooner or later because there is a right time for everything. But we can miss it if we are not "there" for the experience.

It takes courage to move from chaos to the desired state. When you have one foot teetering in the old paradigm and the other in the new, you are very much off balance. If you are willing to remain strong in your resolve, the "off balance" feeling subsides and you are more confident in the new state. It is tempting during the early part of the third stage to want to fix things or return things to "normal." You may be prone to making impulsive decisions if you don't think things are going well.

To continue to grow in the new state you must be willing to:

- Be patient with yourself

- Stay the course

- Get to know the new "you" and how this turning point has influenced your values and beliefs — what you deeply care about

- Reframe your old fears as excitement and opportunity

- Learn to enjoy the "imbalance"—live with the paradoxes

- Maintain the passion and courage

- Continue to engage in breakthrough thinking

- Know that it is not over and another change is likely just around the corner

Life is a series of "bustin' loose" experiences — some so small you don't even feel them and they don't register on the Richter scale. Others are full-blown earthquakes with all of the requisite pain and turmoil. Open yourself to the quakes, both large and small. It is from the pain that the joy will emerge, maybe when you least expect it.

> *All change is a miracle to contemplate; but it is a miracle, which is taking place every instant.*
>
> Henry David Thoreau

Parting Thoughts

Life for baby boomers in the 21st century is not going to be a "bed of roses." For those of us who thought we could just find a good paying job and coast for the duration, we have had a rude awakening in the past couple of decades. Radical change is the order of the day. Many before me have written about the magnitude of change that our world and, in particular, our work world, have been experiencing. It seems, though, that we cannot get too much advice on strategies for managing change. It is just that hard and harder, I think, for baby boomers, who are forced to endure the biggest shift in our thinking and way of being. Our economy needs us baby boomers. It cannot succeed without us, but it needs us to show up differently in the way we think about ourselves and our work.

We need to generate financial success, but we also need to reframe the personal success model to include integrity, passion, and being true to oneself. We need to rekindle some of the spark and gumption we had in the '60s and '70s when we were not afraid to take a stand, make a change, or take big risks to defend our beliefs. We may have lost sight of what our beliefs really are, but it is not too late to reclaim our souls and change the tenor of society. It is up to us.

We must look deep inside for our answers. The external clutter clouds our ability to focus on what we know in the depths of our being. The day-to-day intrusions, diversions, and unexpected events cause us to lose sight of what is important. It is not about pleasing the boss or competing for the next promotion; it is about finding your passion and the place where you can present your best self. This can only happen when you know yourself—mind, body and spirit, believe in a higher source of power, and are willing to unleash your uniqueness.

You can start your personal transformation journey today. You owe it to yourself to unleash your latent potential. You can "bust loose" from the shackles that keep you from being your authentic, best self—the glue that keeps you stuck in unfulfilling endeavors, the box that won't let your light reveal itself, and the mind that has narrowed so much that it obliterates your soul.

Remember: "I am what I am and I am all that I am and I am it." You were miraculously conceived and endowed with unique gifts. Maybe you have gotten your values and priorities confused in this post-modern capitalistic America. It is never too late to get back on the path—your path.

Wishing you peace and blessings along the way.

> **Affirmation:** I will do the thing that I think I cannot do

Summary of Key Points:

- Change is hard.

- Change is inevitable.

- Prepare yourself for constant change.

- Expect more "big" changes.

- Take personal responsibility for managing your own functioning.

- It is natural to resist change.

- There are three stages of change: (1) identification of the need or desire; (2) the transition or chaos phase; (3) and the new state, called "bustin' loose."

- You choose your response to change.

- You will "bust loose" when you free your soul to join you in the journey.

Ask Yourself:

1. How can I stay in the constant state of "I'm ready"?

2. If I lost my job tomorrow, do I know what I would do?

3. How do I experience the transitions from one change stage to another?

4. Am I ready to take the journey of personal transformation?

5. Do I believe that I have abundantly more potential if I could only get over my fear of change?

6. Am I strong in my faith?

7. When will I do the thing that I think I cannot do?

Notes

Introduction

1. "Report PHC T-9. Population by Age, Sex, Race, and Hispanic or Latino Origin for the United States: 2000," *United States Census 2000* 18 February 2002 <http://www.census.gov/>.

2. "Age: 2000, Census 2000 Brief," *United States Census 2000* 18 February 2002 <http://www.census.gov/>.

3. "Report A-14. Employment Status of the Civilian Noninstitutional Population By Age, Sex, and Race," *Bureau of Labor Statistics* 22 February 2002 <ftp://ftp.bls.gov/pub/suppl/empsit.cpseea14.txtftp://ftp.bls.gov/pub/suppl/empsit.cpseea14.txt>.

4. Juliet Schor, *The Overspent American: Upscaling, Downshifting and the New Consumer* (New York: Basic Books, 1998) 20.

5. "In Brief: How Americans Save," *AARP* March 1999, 26 February 2002 <http://research.aarp.org/consume/inb12_save.html>.

6. Allison Bell, "Survey Says Boomers Keep Old Retirement Strategies," *National Underwriter Life and Health-Financial Services Edition* 3 December 2001.

7. "More Americans Dissatisfied with Their Jobs," *The Conference Board* 16 October 2000, 20 February 2002 <www.conference-board.org>.

8. "Table P-1. Historical Income Tables — People," *United States Census 2000* 13 December 2000 <http://www.census.gov/>.

9. "Employee Benefits in Medium and Large Firms: 1989," *Bureau of Labor Statistics, Bulletin 2363* April 2001 <http://www.bls.gov/>.

10. "Employee Benefits in Medium and Large Establishments: 1997," *Bureau of Labor Statistics, News,* USDL 99-02 7 January 1999 <http://www.bls.gov/>.

11. "Work Related Homicides: The Facts," Produced by the Office of Safety, Health and Working Conditions, Spring 2000, *Bureau of Labor Statistics 22* February 2002 <http://www.bls.gov/opub/cwc/2000/Spring/art1full.pdf>.

12. "Top Security Threats, 2001" *Pinkerton* 26 February 2002 <http://www.pinkertons.com/threatsurvey/index.asp>.

Chapter 1

1. Stacy Poulos and Demetra Smith Nightingale, *The Aging Baby Boom: Implications for Employment and Training Programs.* Prepared for the US Department of Labor, Employment and Training Administration, 1995, 18 February 2002 < http://www.urban.org/aging/abb/agingbaby.html >.

2. "Age: 2000, Census 2000 Brief."

3. "Report PHC T-9. Population by Age, Sex, Race, and Hispanic or Latino Origin for the United States: 2000."

4. "Baby Boomers Envision Their Retirement: An AARP Segmentation Analysis," *AARP* 1999 February, 18 February 2002 <http://research.aarp.org/econ/boomer_seg_1.html>.

5. "Annual U.S. Motor Vehicle Sales Report," American Automobile Manufacturers Association.

6. "More Americans Dissatisfied with Their Jobs."

7. "Aging Boomers Refuse to Quit," *Del Webb Corporation*
   3 November 1999, April 2001 <http://www.delwebb.com>.

8. "Baby Boomers Envision Their Retirement: An AARP
   Segmentation Analysis."

Chapter 2

1. William J. Hussar, "Predicting the Need for Newly
   Hired Teachers in the United States 2008-09," *Education
   Statistics Quarterly, Elementary and Secondary Education,*
   1998, 27 February 2002
   <http://nces.ed.gov/pubs99/1999026.pdf>.

2. Arlene Dohm, "Gauging the Labor Force Effects of
   Retiring Baby-boomers," *Monthly Labor Review* July 2000,
   27 February 2002
   <http://www.bls.gov/opub/mlr/2000/07/art2full.pdf>.

3. National Center for Education Statistics, April 2001
   <http://nces.ed.gov/pubs98/98039.pdf.>.

4. Jane Lampman, "Where Are the Young Clergy?" *Christian
   Science Monitor,* 19 July 2001
   <http://csmonitor.com/2001/0719/p15s1-uscu.html>.

5. "The Study of the Impact of Fewer Priests on the Pastoral
   Ministry, Priestly Life and Ministry," *United States
   Conference of Catholic Bishops,* June 2000
   <http://www.usccb.org/plm/summary.htm>.

6. S. Plous, "Ten Myths About Affirmative Action,"
   Journal of Social Issues Winter 1996, April 2001
   <http://www.socialpsychology.org>.

7. *Bureau of Labor Statistics, U.S. Department of Labor,*
   April 2001, 20 February 2002 <http://www.bls.gov/>.

8. "American Federation of Teachers Survey and Analysis of Teacher Salary Trends, 1999," *aft.org* 18 February 2002 <http://www.aft.org/research/survey99/index.html>.

9. "Table 255: Master's Degrees Conferred by Degree-Granting Institutions, By Discipline Division: 1970-71 to 1997-98," *Digest of Education Statistics 2000* 24 February 2002 <http://nces.ed.gov/pubs2001/digest/dt255.html>.

10. Howard Smead, *Don't Trust Anyone Over Thirty: A History of the Baby Boom* (iUniverse, Incorporated, 2000).

11. "Michael Milken," *The Columbia Encyclopedia Online,* Sixth Edition, 2001, 20 February 2002 <http://www.bartleby.com/65/mi/Milken-M.html>.

12. Louis R. Mizell, *Masters Of Deception: The Worldwide White-Collar Crime Crisis and Ways to Protect Yourself* (New York: J. Wiley & Sons, 1997) 101, 126.

13. Louis R. Mizell, 2.

14. "New Era Founder Pleads No Contest to Defrauding Nonprofit Groups," *United Methodist News Service,* Worldwide Faith News archives 31 March 1997, 16 February 2002 <www.wfn.org>.

15. Louis R. Mizell, 99.

16. "Federal Reserve Statistical Release G.19 Consumer Credit Historical Data" 28 February 2002 <http://www.federalreserve.gov>.

17. "Inflation Rates," *The Financial Forecast Center* 12 February 2002 <http://www.forecasts.org/>.

18. "Archived Mass Layoffs," *Bureau of Labor Statistics, U.S. Department of Labor,* December 2000-April 2001, 20 February 2002 <http://www.bls.gov/mls/home.htm>.

19. *CBSMarketWatch* 20 April 2001
    <http://cbs.marketwatch.com/news/economy/layoffs>.

20. "National Population Projections. Projections of the
    Total Resident Population...2025-2040," *U.S. Census
    Bureau* 20 February 2002
    <http://www.census.gov/population/projections/nation/
    summary/np-t3-f.txt>.

21. "Social Security. What is the Approximate Ratio of
    Workers to Beneficiaries?" *The Office of Policy*
    22 February 2002 <www.ssa.gov>.

22. "Ratio of Social Security Covered Workers to Beneficiaries
    Calendar Years 1940-2000," *The Office of Policy*
    22 February 2002 <www.ssa.gov>.

Chapter 3

1. Rushworth M. Kidder, *Shared Values for a Troubled World*
   (San Francisco: Jossey-Bass Inc., 1994) 18-19.

2. "Bowen Theory" 23 February 2002
   <http://www.georgetownfamilycenter.org/pages/theory.
   html>.

Chapter 4

1. Claudia Wallis, "Medicine, Faith and Healing: Can Prayer,
   Faith and Spirituality Really Improve Your Physical
   Health?" *Time Magazine* 24 June 1996: 58-65.

2. Robert B. Reich, *The Future of Success* (New York. Alfred A.
   Knopf, 2000) 111-112.

Chapter 5

1. Kelly Greene, "Terrorist Attacks Spur Americans to Produce Wills," *The Wall Street Journal* 25 September 2001: B7A.

2. "Consumer Fact Sheets: Wills and Living Trusts," *AARP* 11 February 2002 <http://www.aarp.org/confacts/money/wills-trusts.html>.

3. Myers-Briggs Type Indicator (MBTI) and MBTI are registered trademarks and Myers-Briggs is a trademark of Consulting Psychologists Press, Inc.

4. Paul D. Tieger and Barbara Barron-Tieger, *Do What You Are: Discover the Perfect Career for You Through the Secrets of Personality Type* (Boston: Little, Brown and Company, 1992).

5. Kathy Kolbe, *Pure Instinct: Business' Untapped Resource* (New York: Times Books, Random House, 1993).

Chapter 6

1. "Injuries, Illnesses and Fatalities," *Bureau of Labor Statistics, U.S. Department of Labor* 26 February 2002 <http://www.bls.gov/iif/peoplebox.htm#faqd>.

2. Fritz Heider, *The Psychology of Interpersonal Relations* (New Jersey: Erlbaum, 1958).

Chapter 8

1. Daniel H. Pink, *Free Agent Nation* (New York. Warner Books Inc., 2001) 44-45.

2. "The State of Minority Business — Executive Summary, September 21, 2001," *Minority Business Development Agency* 24 February 2002 <http://www.mbda.gov/documents/ smobe_exec_revised.pdf>.

3. Theresa Forsman, "Sizing Up Women-Owned Businesses," *Business Week Online* 16 April 2001, 24 February 2002 <http://www.businessweek.com>.

4. Daniel H. Pink.

Chapter 9

1. "What Work Requires of Schools: A SCANS Report for America 2000. The Secretary's Commission on Achieving Necessary Skills," *US Department of Labor,* June 1991, 24 February 2002 <http://wdr.doleta.gov/SCANS/what work/whatwork.html>.

Chapter 10

1. Michael Beer and Nitin Nohria, "Cracking the Code of Change," *Harvard Business Review,* May-June 2000 <http://www.hbsp.harvard.edu/products/hbr/mayjun00/ R00301.html>

About the Author

Mary-Frances Winters chose to ignore the advice of the Niagara Falls, New York, high school counselor who told her that attending a four-year college was "too lofty" a goal for her as an African American. She entered the University of Rochester in 1969, majoring in English and psychology. Later, she received an M.B.A. and became the University's first African-American female trustee. In 1997, she received an Honorary Doctorate from Roberts Wesleyan College, and in 1998, she was awarded the University of Rochester's prestigious Hutchinson Medal, the highest alumni honor. She has also been a Distinguished Minett Professor at the Rochester Institute of Technology.

Before starting The Winters Group in 1984, Dr. Winters spent 11 years in the corporate arena. She built The Winters Group with clients including not-for-profit agencies, health care organizations and corporations such as Eastman Kodak Company, Xerox Corporation, Mobil, AT&T, United Way, Landmark Communications, and the Council on Foundations. In 1988, she was recognized as the Minority Business Person of the Year in Rochester, followed by the Athena Award from the Women's Council of the Greater Rochester Chamber of Commerce, and the national Women of Enterprise Award from Avon Products, Inc. and the U.S. Small Business Administration. In 1994, Rochester's Urban League presented Dr. Winters with the Outstanding Community Leader Award, and in 1996, her leadership was recognized when she was chosen to carry the Olympic Torch through her hometown. In 1997, the U.S. Small Business Administration named her the Rochester Small Business Person of the Year.

Dr. Winters contributes regularly to Gannett Newspapers' *USA Today* and *Democrat and Chronicle* and a number of professional journals. She has published a journal titled *Unleashing Your True Potential in the Workplace: A Journal for Self-Discovery and Unprecedented Performance* and is often a featured speaker on issues affecting the workplace and diversity. She is a member of the National Speakers' Association.

To contact Mary-Frances Winters, e-mail
mfwinters@wintersgroup.com
or write to her at:
The Winters Group, 8816 Jericho City Drive,
Landover, MD 20785

To order more copies of
Only Wet Babies Like Change, go to:
www.Laniersbookstore.com
www.wintersgroup.com
or call ***(301) 336-0400***